The other side of
BROADWAY

A young producer's journey through New York theatre in the 1970s and '80s, launching Howard Ashman, learning from Hal Prince, and coping with the colorful insanity of a bygone era.

a theatre memoir by
STEPHEN WELLS

ISBN: 979-8-993-52060-5

Published by Fiver Publications

*For my sons, Andrew and David, with the hope that you follow
your passions as well, wherever they may lead you*

Author's Note

This memoir is in roughly chronological order, except in the instances that I relate the story of a show's development, I do so in full, regardless of the point in time when the project either ended or reached fruition. In some of these cases, I will have moved on from the professional base I had when I started developing it. So the chronological order is from the beginning of each chapter, not necessarily the end.

Many of the quotes are exact. However, given the passage of time, some may not be exactly as they were spoken, but all are very close to, and fully capture the essence of, what was said at the time.

And a note for younger readers: While the dollar amounts mentioned may seem small compared to today, trust me that they were significant at the time.

Preface

Whenever a young person wanting to go into professional theatre asks me for advice, I've always had a simple answer for them:

If there's any other occupation that you think you'd find fulfilling, forget theatre.

Of course, I tell them why I say that, and the reason is simple. If their passion isn't so deep, so unshakable, so singular, so much part of their being that they can't imagine doing anything else, then they'll never be able to endure the uncertainties, the failures, the disappointments, the long periods of inactivity, and the probable financial stresses.

On top of all that, it's much more difficult today than when I was young and knew no one in New York theatre who might help me get started. And once you do get started, you have to be prepared for more failures than successes, often through no fault of your own; in fact, much of your best work will be on shows that fail. And, unlike most professions, those failures will be public. None of a doctor's friends, say, are aware if he or she makes a critical misdiagnosis or botches a surgery, but yours are all aware if *The New York Times* pans a show you've done.

If, given those warnings, the young person proceeds anyway, I give them my full encouragement and support, for whatever good that does them.

Sometimes the real world will impose barriers to them achieving their initial passions and they'll have to adapt them in one way or another, as eventually happened to me and many others, including the late Howard Ashman, who figures prominently in this memoir because of my close association with him in our early professional years. But then most professions require their practitioners to adapt to changing realities, most often brought about by economics, technology, shifting cultures, or a combination of all three.

In fact, I've come realize that many of the emotional and professional vicissitudes I went through are, at their core, no different than what those in other professions experience:

Being disappointed by people you had admired from afar.

Being thrilled when someone older and greatly respected recognizes you as a colleague.

Wondering how your boss was ever hired and feeling you could do his job better.

Heartbreak when something you've strived for doesn't work out.

Joy when it does.

So my hope is that this memoir will have resonance for people who may not be involved with or interested in professional theatre, as well, of course, as those who are.

What follows is a candid recollection of my roughly quarter-century in New York theatre. As I look back to my beginnings, I recall one of my drama professors in college telling me "You're not as advanced as you think you are." In retrospect, he was probably right. But if I hadn't been unshakeable then in my belief that I *was*, in fact, ready to swim in the deep end, I never would have dived in, headfirst.

Besides, I knew in my heart that I had no choice. It was way too much part of my being.

Rolling the Dice in My Twenties

On the Corner of 2nd & Main

I had become obsessed with Broadway during my freshman year of high school. A psychologist might speculate that it provided me an escape from my troubled adolescence, with my father in a turbulent second marriage, my mother living in the past and being emotionally dependent on me, and my all-boys school contributing to my retarded social development. But all I knew was that I couldn't wait for each weekend to roll around so I could see the next Broadway play or musical, usually in the company of my mother.

I started writing reviews and took them more seriously than my schoolwork. I developed a rapport with an English teacher who would give me assessments of them, as would a family friend who had once been in the business. I'd submit one of them to appear in each issue of the school paper. Clive Barnes was the *Times* critic then, and "Clive" soon became my high school nickname. When my cliché-ridden rave review of "Mame" ran in the paper, I sent a copy to Angela Lansbury, who wrote me a lovely note of appreciation on her light blue, personalized, onion skin stationery.

By the time I began college at the University of Virginia, I had my mind set on a future career as a drama critic. I joined the daily student newspaper, *The Cavalier Daily*, right away. To my delight, I was put in the position of drama critic immediately. I reviewed University productions, films that played at local theatres, and Broadway shows for the next three years.

But over that time, I started reading and admiring the work of another aspiring drama critic who was a student at Harvard and wrote for its paper, *The Crimson*. He had a sophistication of both insight and language that I didn't, and, as hard as I tried, I couldn't bring my writing up to his level. I knew I was good, but it bothered me that I wasn't as good as Frank Rich.

Rich's review of the Boston tryout of "Follies" had put him on everyone's radar as an exceptional writing talent. I later learned just how similar our backgrounds and introductions to Broadway theatre had been, even down to our divorced mothers smoking the same brand of cigarettes, but at this juncture all I knew was that, doing my best, I could only be second best.

In my final year at Virginia, I became editor-in-chief of *The Cavalier Daily* and, due to the all-consuming responsibilities of that position, phased myself out of drama criticism. Then, at some point that year, I received an offer from the manager of the main downtown movie theatre who was one of our most reliable advertisers. He wanted to do two midnight showings one weekend of the 1936 propaganda film that ludicrously exaggerates the dangers of marijuana, "Reefer Madness." His proposal was that *The Cavalier Daily* would guarantee his parent company, ABC Southeastern Theatres, $1,000 and we would keep any gross receipts above that number. ABC Southeastern would take no risk and get as much free advertising as we wanted to provide. Of course, if the two showings fell short of grossing $1,000, we'd have to absorb the loss.

I accepted the deal without hesitation. I smelled a winner. 1972, college kids, late night, laughable cult film of bygone days… all the factors felt right. Now all we had to do was make it work.

The University, however, got wind of the deal I had made and flipped out. The Dean of Student Affairs was irate that I'd gamble with University monies that had been partly generated from student activities fees and wanted me to try to nullify the arrangement. He calmed down a bit when I said that, if he wanted, I would personally cover any potential losses. But when I added, "Of course, that means I personally get any potential profits, too," he became all but incoherent.

I was loving this. I wasn't focused on the money, but the *game*. He had no idea what to do or say, fearful that accepting my offer could backfire on him. He said he'd get back to me. Which he never did.

We moved forward and promoted the hell out of the midnight shows through feature stories and large display ads. Our goal was to make sure every student at the University knew about the event and would view it as a cool thing to do.

When I saw the crowd entering for the Friday night screening, I figured we'd be in pretty good shape. It turned out to be better than that. We did over $900 at the box office. Close to aggregate breakeven. Whatever we did the next night would basically be gravy.

The next night, Saturday, I came up 2nd Street approaching the Paramount Theatre. And when I reached the corner, I saw the line. Going down Main Street. Around the corner. Down *that* block. I couldn't see the end of it.

I leapt in the air and felt a rush of euphoria unlike any sensation I had ever experienced in school, sports, or journalism. I was hooked. I knew I had to seek that feeling in my professional career in order to be fulfilled.

It was never about the money. In fact, it never became about the money for me. (Probably a fortunate mindset since my biggest career successes were in the not-for-profit sector.) It was about the joy of winning, of proving the doubters wrong, of making something worthwhile possible, whether it be an enriching experience for people or simply a couple of hours of fun.

The two midnight showings of "Reefer Madness" grossed about $2,500, or $1,500 above the $1,000 guarantee. In 1972, that was, of course, much more meaningful in real dollars than it is today, and the home office of ABC Southeastern Theatres took note of the profits they had signed away. I received a letter from the regional manager confirming the amount of the excess and saying we'd shortly be receiving a check for $750 based on our agreed-upon fifty-fifty split of profits.

Whoa, Nellie! Not so fast, buddy boy. That wasn't our deal. There's a little thing called a contract giving us *all* box office proceeds over the $1,000 guarantee. They must have thought we were some dumb kids who had no idea what we had signed. I quickly blew away their feeble revisionist ploy, copying the newspaper's attorney on my response. They caved without much of a fight. I subsequently got to know the regional manager who tried to take advantage of us and I'm convinced that the respect I felt coming from him was *because* I had stood up to him. For me, it was good training for the type of stunts I'd have to deal with in the business of New York theatre.

When the check for the full amount arrived, we deposited it directly into the newspaper's account. I never did hear anything more from the Student Affairs office, not so much as a "Well done!" or "Congratulations!" or "Thank you." But I didn't need that. I had my indelible memory of that Saturday evening in downtown Charlottesville, on the street corner across from the Paramount.

Winging It

It was the summer of 1973 and political corruption dominated the public consciousness. Almost every day a meeting of the Senate Watergate Committee was blaring from televisions on all three networks. Resignations and prosecutions related to Watergate dominated newspapers, as did new revelations from *The Washington Post*'s Bernstein/Woodward duo. Watergate was ubiquitous. There was no escaping it.

It was in this climate that 29-year-old University of Virginia drama professor Buzz McLaughlin and graduate student Peter Ryan adapted Aristophanes' "The Birds" to present as a student production that summer. The story of two men fleeing from their corrupt ancient Athens society to create a (supposedly) purer one with the feathered species had particular resonance at the time. And Buzz and Peter's choice to add music, in the form of their own bouncy original score, gave it a liveliness that put it in the same genre as "Godspell," which had become an off-Broadway sensation only two years before.

So where do I fit into all this? Well, I happened to be finishing up my college degree requirements at U.Va. that summer but was spending most of my time figuring out how to break into New York theatre. Having run a newspaper with a six-figure budget for most of the prior year, I (perhaps unreasonably) wanted to start my theatre career as something more than somebody's gofer. But I was totally stumped as to how to do it. (Surely by now you see where this is headed.)

I tried to push the thoughts I was having about "The Birds" out of my mind. I knew I had to resist the temptation. It was impractical. Too soon. Required more experience. Having read a few books on producing and being well-versed in New York theatre from the outside wouldn't be enough.

Yet I had been bitten by the bug.

My father had tragically died in my junior year of high school and I knew I'd be inheriting some money in the near future once his estate was finally settled. The inheritance wouldn't be enough to make me wealthy but would definitely be sufficient to give me a financial cushion as I started my career, even if I wanted to do something insanely ambitious like attempting to produce a show in New York.

Given this, I somehow convinced myself that I could probably raise the $100,000 I figured would be necessary to produce the musical off-Broadway and thought of people I could target to invest in it. (As it turned out, none of those people were among the 108 investors we finally landed.)

I should have known better, but I was blinded to the improbability of the mission I was about to embark on. I trusted my instincts and was ready to fly by the proverbial seat of my pants.

Once Buzz and Peter got over their initial incredulousness at what I was proposing, they were enthusiastic and ready to move forward. I drew up a boilerplate option agreement, gave them $500, and we were on our way.

The two authors spent the fall doing rewrites, refining what already existed and adding new material. They also gave the show a new title: "Wings." It was a title that had been used before (and has been since), but it fit the show perfectly. They then crafted a title song that, well, soared. Meanwhile, in the outside world, Watergate showed no signs of ending, with Agnew having been forced to resign the vice-presidency and Nixon engineering the Saturday Night Massacre.

By December, Buzz and Peter's work was done and it was time for me to hire a theatrical attorney. I made a cold inquiry by letter and got an immediate response by phone. We set a meeting for early January, after which the necessary papers were drawn up and filed with the SEC and New York State Attorney General's office, allowing me to sell shares in a limited partnership we called The Birds Company.

Part of this process was hiring a general manager and we were fortunate to have been referred to Bill Craver, who was a joy to work with and whom I would subsequently refer to as my mentor, which he always scoffed at but which was true. I was learning from the top down rather than the bottom up. (Shortly after "Wings," Craver switched his career focus to representing writers and directors and became a distinguished theatre lit agent with whom I had many future nonsense-free dealings.)

In March of 1974, we started staging backers' auditions, first in New York City, then in Charlottesville, using five or six performers in each. We realized two things pretty quickly. First, less is more. Auditions with the two authors (and sometimes one or two female singers) performing the songs were much more effective than more elaborate presentations. Secondly, it was much harder raising money in New York, where theatre investors were being hit up all the time, than in Virginia, where the concept of investing in a theatre production was a novelty. So, with the help of several "associate producers," each of whom would get a share of potential profits based on how many investors they introduced us to, we barnstormed Virginia and, eventually, North Carolina for the remainder of that spring and summer.

It was a grind, and, at times, I thought we had hit a brick wall and would have to admit failure. But somehow, each time this happened, we soon found another pool of prospective investors to tap into. We perfected the backers' presentations, which began receiving coverage in local newspapers and on television.

In all, it took us six months and 20 backers' auditions to raise the full capitalization, all from small investors (our biggest was

$2,500). By September, we were fully capitalized and began filling out the production team.

Early on, we had retained a colleague of Buzz's at U.Va. to direct. (As I think he was basically a decent person, we'll simply call him George.) Buzz himself wisely didn't want to stay on as director, and George's inventive student production of "Volpone" the previous year had garnered raves from industry professionals such as Alan Schneider and had been selected to play in the annual American College Theatre Festival at the Kennedy Center. Creatively, he seemed perfect, and I (perhaps unwisely) wasn't bothered by the fact that he didn't have any New York experience.

Similarly, we hired the U.Va. faculty member who, on a $300 budget, had designed the colorful and striking costumes for the student production. Craver and I had budgeted $3,000 for costumes in New York and I figured that if she created what she did with one-tenth that amount, what she could do with three grand would be mind-boggling.

We sought out the remainder of the creative team in New York. The orchestrator was perhaps the hardest to land. We met with Hayward Morris, who had done excellent work on "Your Own Thing" and whom we thought would be perfect, but he said he had gotten a $6,000 fee on that show and we were only offering $3,000. Somehow we found our way to Bill Brohn, a top-tier orchestrator who was creatively intrigued by our show and wasn't fazed by the small fee. Despite his stature and warm demeanor, I wasn't sure he was 100% right for a soft rock musical, but Buzz and Peter really wanted him, so I ignored the little voice in the back of my head. We then hired as musical director an impressive – and impressively educated – 21-year-old named Larry Hochman, who himself would go on to successfully join the ranks of career Broadway orchestrators.

When we held our first round of auditions, in a small theatre space near Union Square, George said he couldn't be there due to commitments in Charlottesville, but he'd definitely make it for call-backs. He trusted us to make the initial round of cuts.

The auditions themselves were mostly uneventful, except for one actress who refused to stop singing. After a respectable amount of time, Buzz said "thank you," yet she kept on going. I signaled Hochman to stop accompanying her. She kept right on. Becoming annoyed, I gave her the "throat cut" signal to stop. She gave the "throat cut" back to me. Finally, she stopped and proceeded to lecture us on how we hadn't heard her reach her final octave when we told her to stop. Perhaps needless to say, she didn't get a callback.

We held the next two rounds of auditions in mid-December in rehearsal studios next door to the Lunt-Fontanne. We had to move quickly because George could only be there for a few days. On the first morning, the guy who ran the place, who could have passed for Quasimodo's older brother, barfed right in front of the entrance as he was unlocking the door for George. (Maybe he knew something we didn't.)

The callbacks went smoothly for the most part. The show called for a cast of 15, which was large for off-Broadway. But it required youthful talent, which is the easiest type to find. I did have two clashes with George, though. When we cast the lead, an unknown named Jerry Sroka, he took George and me aside and nervously told us that his wife had been given a callback audition as well and said he'd appreciate it if we could hire her, too. Granted, this was unprofessional on Sroka's part, and George told him no, she wasn't likely to be cast. I remained silent because I considered it George's call, but we wouldn't have lost anything creatively by hiring his wife, and the politics of the situation might have suggested a different response since so much was riding on Sroka's performance.

The second clash was over the casting of one of the main roles. The choice seemed clear to me. An actor named Douglas Hayle came in and had us all cracking up at his comic inventiveness. I was shocked when George said he preferred an actor in whom I saw no personality. The authors agreed with me, but we all deferred to George.

Rehearsals were soon upon us, which means those of you reading this who are musical theatre sadists are in for a treat. Let the nightmare begin.

In the pre-production period, we again had trouble getting George out of Virginia; seems his wife was somehow involved with an upcoming student production of "Guys and Dolls" and George had to be there to take care of their kids.

Huh? A college production was taking priority over a new off-Broadway musical about to go into rehearsal?

George did have telephone conversations with the set designer of his choosing, the accomplished Karl Eigsti, and he at least agreed to come to New York for a day to see Eigsti's finished product. We arrived at Karl's studio one Sunday afternoon, and he unveiled the model for his set. To say it was elaborate would be an understatement; it even had a running waterfall. I immediately said it was impractical for an off-Broadway budget, and Karl responded that he knew he'd have to cut it back. The problem was that George was catching a flight home to Virginia that night. Eigsti told us to go have an early dinner and he'd redesign it in those few hours, and for us to come back after we ate to see it. Over a year of my life (not to mention Buzz and Peter's) killing myself to get to this point, and the set is being designed while we have a quick bite at Brew'n Burger?

To his credit, Eigsti pulled it off. His revised set was very workable and affordable. And, most important, of course, George made it to LaGuardia on time.

I booked the Eastside Playhouse, which Craver happened to manage, and we were able to use the stage for the full rehearsal period. Everything seemed fine for the first ten days. Then one day as I was walking to Craver's office on the second level, it dawned on me that all the staging I had sporadically seen appeared to take place downstage left. I mentioned it to George, who exploded, saying

"You don't judge an artist's painting until it's finished!" Still, it made no sense.

I had also begun noticing that the tempos of the music were lagging. The score's inherent and essential energy was missing. I spoke to Hochman about it, but little changed.

Most disturbingly, I began noticing signs of arrogance and rebellion in the cast. As for their arrogance, it turned out we had hired several of the most insecure young *prima donnas* in New York. In terms of rebellion, the show called for many of them to play birds that were stupid, and the young actors were afraid that if they fully committed themselves to that, they *themselves* would look stupid. But when they held back, nothing worked and they began to panic.

"There is only one kind of clown I cannot tolerate," the critic Walter Kerr once wrote, "and that is the kind who is himself uncommitted to what he is doing."

Often, it's a hard lesson for young actors to learn. About a decade later, Barry Harman, a friend and colleague, was developing a new musical called "Olympus on My Mind" in a workshop production and had cast a young Faith Prince in the show's pivotal, broadly comedic role. He invited me to an early performance, at which the show died. Prince was playing it too straight. She was afraid *she'd* look ridiculous if she committed to making her character look ridiculous. Barry had unsuccessfully tried to prod and reassure her, but nothing worked until he finally got her to reluctantly agree to try it his way for just one performance. The audience responded as hoped, and it turned out several of her friends were at the show that night, all of whom told her afterwards how terrific and funny she was. Lesson learned, and she went on to win accolades and awards playing the ditzy Adelaide in the 1992 Broadway revival of "Guys and Dolls," which launched her successful career. As for "Olympus," I went back a second time; it indeed now clicked on all cylinders and subsequently moved to the Lambs Theatre for an open-ended off-Broadway run.

But, back in early 1975, the cast of "Wings" stubbornly remained their earthbound selves and tensions grew.

Birnam Wood arrived at Dunsinane on a Saturday morning two weeks in. Craver called me at home to say that our choreographer, a fellow named Ronn Forella, had just quit. I bolted up to the theatre and held a no-holds barred summit meeting in Bill's office with the writers, George, Bill, and me. The show was stagnating, the cast wasn't following direction, and the damned stage focus was still perplexingly down left. By the end of the meeting, George was out as director; whether he quit or was fired is a matter of perspective. But he actually seemed relieved. He could now go back to Virginia for good, which seemed to be where his heart was.

I thought it made the most sense that Buzz take over the direction since he had staged the show before and knew exactly what it should be. A replacement for Forella – Nora Peterson, a young woman who the prior year had choreographed Bernsein's "Mass" in Vienna – had been recommended to us; we liked and quickly hired her and moved onward again. Over the following few days, the show that I knew and wanted began to emerge. Even the musical energy improved. There was reason for optimism.

The cast, though, viewed Buzz as fresh meat to devour. We had already lost them and each rehearsal soon became a struggle. One would reasonably expect actors to cut their new director some slack and give him a chance to right the ship, but not this bunch. They had been adrift for too long.

After several days, Buzz began cracking. It didn't help that his co-author, Peter, was badgering him constantly about changing their billing so he would get greater credit for the lyrics (this never happened, nor should it have). Buzz was under attack from all sides. His hallmark energy disappeared and he seemed so close to having a breakdown that I called his wonderfully supportive wife, Kris, in Virginia and told her she needed to get up here.

Unbelievably, we again needed a new director. Nora recommended a recent graduate of the Yale School of Drama whom she knew and admired named Peter Mark Schifter. Schifter went on to achieve a respectable degree of success before he was claimed by AIDS in 1993 at the age of 44 – directing the original production of Albert Innaurato's hit play, "Gemini," among other achievements – but when we hired him, he only made a bad situation worse. He wanted to bring in a writer he knew to do a few rewrites. I didn't see the need for this, but I didn't want to deny him his one request before he even ventured into our war zone. The writer's name was Moose, and the material he started churning out was cringeworthy. Now the cast had another reason to rebel.

In the decades that have ensued, I've often been asked if I thought I would've made the same mistakes had I produced the show later in my career. My answer has always been it's quite possible I would have. The question of waiting too long to change directors, or not long enough, is a matter of judgment specific to each production's circumstances. I always tell those who ask that the only difference had I been faced with the same circumstances 10 years later would have been that I'd have had a bigger Rolodex and would have known who to call for help when I realized we were in trouble. For instance, had it been just a year later, Schifter and Moose never would have seen the inside of our theatre unless they bought tickets; my first and only call would have been to Howard Ashman. But in early 1975, I was still several months away from meeting him.

Anyway, opening night was approaching fast, and we didn't have the financial luxury of postponing it again (I had already pushed it back once). A few days into the new regime, the cast began openly mocking Moose's new material and had begun engaging in open combat with Schifter.

Meanwhile, as the band began rehearsing and we heard Brohn's orchestrations, two things were immediately apparent: they were brilliant and, as I had feared, they were wrong for this show. Buzz and Peter were less emphatic about this; in fact, they only saw the "brilliant" part. I think, as artists, they had heard these songs so many times in the last two years that they enjoyed hearing them in a different way. But, for me, it was more like they were dressed up in Sunday's finest when Sunday's finest isn't what you wear to a pop rock concert. Regardless, it was too late to change.

It was also time for the costume parade. And, in keeping with the other disasters around me, inexplicably the costumes began falling apart *during the parade*. The designer had done fabulous work with $300 a year and a half earlier and now *this* is what we get for 10 times that amount?! Do some people really get that intimidated when working in New York as opposed to the boonies?

Knowing we had to replace her quickly, Karl Eigsti recommended a costume designer he had recently worked with at Arena Stage, a fellow who went simply by "Shadow." (Okay, whatever.) Shadow came to the theatre and we talked about what he'd need to design and execute.

"How long do I have?" Shadow inquired.

"Three days," I replied.

He looked downward and said "Oh, feet, do your stuff."

(Apparently his feet obeyed. His costumes were fine, and on time, although perhaps a bit too stylish for the show.)

Things were quickly deteriorating on stage, moving from bad to worse. When I saw an actor doing a Minnie Pearl impersonation that Schifter and Moose had incorporated into the new material, that was it for me. The situation had become untenable and Moose had to be fired.

I told Schifter and our persevering stage manager, the exceptional Peter Lawrence, that we were going back to the old script. Apparently, Schifter was still hoping to keep at least a few of Moose's improvements and the cast got mixed messages. Sroka came running up to the balcony and office area and confronted me, saying he was going crazy and didn't even know which script to follow. He was screaming as Craver came up the stairs and saw Buzz lying on the floor, trying to tune out the chaos, with his wife, Kris, by his side. Bill's first thought was that Sroka had decked Buzz.

We released the juvenile delinquents – er, cast – for the day, and members of the production team gathered in the balcony. Nora Peterson looked to be in a daze, staring straight ahead at the balcony railing. Her first comment was "I just wish I had the courage to jump."

This was the day that I gave up any hope of salvaging the production. But I was determined to at least get us to opening night. It seemed that the only way to do this was to have one of the few mature, non-problematic actors with a directing background take the helm as a caretaker for the handful of days that remained. Simply put, there was nothing he, nor anyone, could do to change the inevitable outcome this late in the game, and at least we'd have a few days of peace before the show was ignobly relegated to the status of a footnote in New York theatre history.

Investors from the south flew in for opening night. I had asked them to contribute funds for the opening night party rather than include it in the show's budget. And, because of that, we were able to do it right. We rented out the former Act I Restaurant, with a view of all of Times Square from upper floors of the original Times Tower, from which the New Year's Eve ball drops every year.

I had always dreamed of going to the legendary advertising agency Blaine-Thompson in the Sardi Building on an opening night of mine to hear the early reviews, including the *Times*, come in via phone and wire. But my dream never included the dismissive, if deserved, notices we received that night, including from Clive Barnes in the *Times* who ended his saying "Those who enjoy 'Wings' the most will be those who come expecting the least."

Standing in the conference room with Craver, the writers, our ad exec, Mike DeLuise (who became a lifelong friend and colleague), our press agent, Mary Bryant, and all our key personnel, we reached a unanimous decision to close the show after only one performance. We went back to the party, which quickly disbanded, as opening night gatherings usually do when the reviews are bad.

I was up most of the night, with my mind trying to deal both with the show's fate and a nagging personal problem. I had finally fallen asleep when the phone rang. It was Mary Bryant and her first words were "Steve, Martin Gottfried has just written you a money review in the *Post*." My immediate thought was that he must have gone to the wrong theatre. (Part of me still believes that!)

She started reading it to me. I soon realized she was correct: it was an out-and-out rave, with a stream of positive adjectives. What I found most startling about this was that I had always been on the same wavelength as Gottfried. It got to the point that friends would call me to ask my opinion of a show in previews just so they'd know what Gottfried would say about it. This is one of the very few shows I ever disagreed with him on – and it happened to be my own. And we disagreed in a way that was the exact opposite of how one would expect a producer to differ with a critic.

I started walking over to Mary's office in the "Equity building" on the corner of 46th and Seventh, which wasn't easy because it happened to be St. Patrick's Day and I had to cross the parade route on Fifth Avenue, dodging both marchers and the hordes of parade-goers gathering. By the time I arrived, another rave had come in from the critic for United Press International (in those days, wire service reviews were fairly important).

I was totally befuddled. I knew I wasn't wrong about the show not working, but how could these euphoric reactions be ignored? I was aware that Gottfried was a poker pal of our music publisher, but would he really allow himself to be this far off the mark in the vain hope of helping a buddy? And that still wouldn't explain the UPI review.

I realized I didn't have any choice but to keep the show open for the coming week, run quote ads, and see how the box office responded.

Craver called Peter Lawrence and told him the show hadn't closed on opening night after all and to notify the cast that they had a performance that night. Lawrence couldn't believe his ears, but responded professionally as he always did. To this day, I believe we never would have made it to opening night without him. He went on to become Mike Nichols' go-to production stage manager and one of the most sought-after backstage talents on Broadway. I worked with several excellent stage managers through the years, but I regret that the opportunity to work with Peter again never presented itself.

As for "Wings," the amount we spent on *Times* ads quoting Gottfried and UPI that week ended up being more than we grossed at the box office. Thanks to Craver's business acumen, somehow I came out of the fiasco owing only $5,000, despite the loss incurred in the one week of post-opening performances; everything else was able to be covered by the capitalization.

The crucial ingredient in any production, of course, is the most intangible one, and that's chemistry. When "Wings" got to New York, it couldn't find that. Or at least it couldn't find any *good* chemistry. Some of what happened still defies logic, and some of it was due to the dearth of pre-production discussion among all creative personnel so everyone could be working toward a unified vision. And when I saw this not happening, I should have changed directors before we even began casting.

But there was also something else. Have you noticed I haven't made references to Watergate since early in this chapter? When I decided in 1973 to produce this show, the concept behind both Aristophanes' play and this musical couldn't have been more relevant; audiences could easily relate to the desire of the two lead characters to try to escape the corruption and dysfunction of their society. But by the time we opened in New York in 1975, the immediacy of the show's premise had long since vanished. The Watergate scandal was yesterday's news and we were seven months into the era of "straight talk among friends."

Buzz McLaughlin would return to his teaching career and eventually branch out successfully into professional theatre endeavors I'll describe later. Peter Ryan, sadly, would be haunted, perhaps even crippled, by the failure of "Wings," which for years he continued by himself to try to rewrite before he moved on to producing children's theatre in Virginia. And to paraphrase one of Peter Stone's memorable lines in the musical "1776," the cast members moved on to achieve the anonymity most of them so richly deserved.

As for me, I went into a funk. I had no idea how to move on, how to salvage my career. I thought it was over almost before it began and I sank into a deep depression. In retrospect, I obviously realize I was blowing the setbacks in both my professional and personal lives way out of proportion. Still, the drapes of my apartment were shut and, while never suicidal, I was sure I'd never experience the sun shining on my life again.

Such Stuff As Dreams Are Made On

The thing about falling into a life-ending depression at age 25 is that you eventually discover it's the depression, not your life, that ends.

My good friend and gifted lyricist Dennis Green had been writing some songs with a young soft-rock composer from Brooklyn named Marsha Malamet for a musical adaptation of Shakespeare's "The Tempest." He had played a recording of them for me a few times, and, while the songs themselves were impressive, I didn't see how integrating them into Shakespeare's text would make for an exciting, commercially viable show.

But by the spring of 1975, Dennis was telling me how they had started working with a recent graduate of the Masters program at Indiana University named Howard Ashman, who had devised a clever concept for the show and was now writing the book.

The concept Ashman had come up with was indeed unexpected. Call it Neil Simon meets Bill Shakespeare. The shipwrecked characters were Ashman's creations, a family straight out of the New York City garment district, and spoke only *his* words, while the island characters remained true to Shakespeare's text. A further conceit was that none of the shipwrecked characters would sing until he or she had been touched by the island's magic.

The problem I saw was that to pull this off it would take that rarest of creatures: a master bookwriter and musical theatre structuralist. What I, or even Dennis and Marsha, had no way of knowing at the time is that Howard already *was* one.

When the writers had completed a rough draft of the show, Dennis invited me to a private read-through by them at Marsha's small Upper West Side walk-up. I was charmed, and by the end of the evening, I had become part of the team. There was something special about both Howard and Marsha, and I knew I wanted to work with them – in addition, of course, to Dennis.

Marsha's score was at once driving and melodic, as well as distinctive. She freely admitted "I don't know from Shakespeare," and, trust me, she didn't. But somehow when she set two of Shakespeare's lyric fragments written for the sprite Ariel – "Full Fathom Five" and "Where the Bee Sucks" – her composition perfectly and eerily captured the tone and meaning of his words while remaining of a piece with the show's contemporary sound.

As they continued to develop and refine the material, it became clear that Howard was guiding the ship. It didn't take me long to be impressed by his eagerness to edit his own writing, advocate that songs be cut and replaced where necessary, and tweak the show's structure in ways that assured its motor wouldn't have a single sputter.

Howard wanted a breezy title for the show, a one-word description of it that, like "Godspell," might not be an existing word at all but which captured the essence of the material. We kicked around several possibilities over many weeks, and finally Dennis came up with the one we agreed on: "Dreamstuff."

We then discussed initial production steps. Howard had a friend named Jim Nicola who was looking for a new musical to direct the following spring at the WPA Theatre, which was then located in the Bowery. Nicola (who went on to successfully run New York Theater Workshop, which launched "Rent") was interested. If I'd be willing to put up a few thousand dollars to supplement WPA's budget, it could all happen. I was and it did.

During rehearsals, we began to sense we indeed had something magical on our hands. Two members of the WPA's board of directors, who had independently co-produced the original off-Broadway production of "Dames at Sea," thought so too and began hovering. But I had the commercial rights tightly locked up and wouldn't have parted with them for anything. The WPA ran out of money during rehearsals, and my enthusiasm was so high that I lent them a few thousand more to get through.

The one glitch in rehearsals was when the costumes arrived the week before we opened it was painfully evident that WPA's designer had made them out of plastic garbage bags. (An inexplicable costume disaster *again?!*) We scrambled. As part of our scrambling, I gave Howard my credit card to take the actor David Lipman – the human embodiment of the Pillsbury Doughboy – to Bloomingdale's to buy him the type of tacky vacation clothes a mid-level garment district executive would wear. The image of Howard dashing around Bloomie's, outfitting Lipman, still brings a smile to my face.

We began assembling the pieces to be ready for a commercial transfer. I had a general manager and press agent in place, and Chappell Music had already flipped over the score and given Marsha and Dennis a publishing deal. We just needed the critics – Clive Barnes of the *Times* in particular – to give their blessing. When we began performances, audiences almost immediately responded as enthusiastically as we had hoped, with both laughter and generous applause every night.

But the critics didn't play their part in our dream. The best Clive Barnes could say in his mixed-to-negative review was that the show was "occasionally fair fun." Now there's a *Times* money quote to sell a show on! Chapman's review in the *Daily News* was headlined "Tempest in a Shoebox" and it went downhill from there. Maybe we hadn't moved the Bowery winos far enough away from the theatre's doorstep to suit him.

Simply put, as a group, the critics were in a "don't tamper with my Shakespeare" mood, whereas with the earlier "Two Gentlemen of Verona" they had adopted a "take as many liberties as you want" kind of attitude. Why is Shakespeare sacrosanct in one instance and not in another? (Remember: the only rationale is there's no rationale.)

Most ironically, among the major New York critics of the day, even "Wings" had fared better than "Dreamstuff," which made no sense at all.

Audiences continued to come to the remaining two weeks of scheduled performances, and the reaction was every bit as positive as the reception that preview audiences had given the show. But the heat around it had disappeared. As far as a possible commercial move was concerned, we had no ammo to overcome the reviews.

At moments like these, you try to convince yourself the ballgame isn't *really* lost, that the dream hasn't truly died. Howard had decided that the problem with the production was Jim Nicola, the director. For once, I didn't agree with him, and I was basing that on Jim's work and trying to put aside that he was one of nicest guys you'd ever want to meet. But I didn't want the show to die any more than Howard and the others did.

A few years before, I had been impressed with several aspects of Jon Jory's staging of a short-lived Broadway musical called "Tricks," a small show based on a Moliere farce that had been mounted in too large a theatre. By that time, Jory had developed a strong regional reputation as Artistic Director of Actors Theatre of Louisville. I flew him in from Kentucky, he saw our show, and then he and I met the following morning. He wasn't the least bit critical of Nicola's staging and said he didn't know what he would do differently. His take was that we had just gotten a bad break with the critics, much as he had with "Tricks" (although I believe "Dreamstuff" to have been a far superior show). We later discovered that, by pure coincidence, he was good friends with Nicola's boss at Jim's then-current New York Shakespeare Festival day job, and had had pre-theatre dinner with her the night before, apparently having no idea of the connection. Such is the small world of professional theatre. Still, I agreed with his assessment.

Regardless, when we ended the run at the WPA on the Bowery, we knew it was the end of the line. Even though Howard had grown to vehemently dislike some of the cast members (as I would come to learn was standard for him), they were a talented group who were committed to the show and enjoyed being in it – a distinct pleasure for me after "Wings." Sadly, less than two years later at age 27, our Miranda, a naturally pretty and personable ingenue named Debbie Weems, who also was a semi-regular on the kids' tv series "Captain Kangaroo," jumped out of her 16th floor apartment window to her death. We had never seen her without a smile on her face.

A Confirmation Under Fire

At the same time the prospects of a Broadway move for "Dream-stuff" were fading and causing dismay among those of us who were passionate about it, a new potential passion appeared on my horizon, courtesy of Howard Ashman.

Within walking distance of the WPA in the East Village, Circle Repertory Company was presenting a workshop of a semi-autobiographical play Howard had written entitled "The Confirmation," which was a candid, somewhat critical and ultimately mournful depiction of his family from his days growing up in a row house in lower-middle class Baltimore where, to quote one of the play's lines, "my house looks like your house looks like their house looks like nothing."

Howard omitted himself as a character, leaving a father, mother, and 15-year-old daughter as the nuclear family at the center. Although the title deals with the play's pending event – the daughter's confirmation celebration – the primary focus of the piece is the father, who refuses to accept, or even see, that his world, anchored in Judaism, is changing and his life's meaning slipping away.

The Circle workshop was directed by Howard's long-time partner at the time, Stuart White, as sweet and gentle a soul as I had ever met. And incredibly gifted at his craft. His was anything but a vanity assignment.

When I first saw the production in workshop, I was engrossed throughout and extremely moved at the end. Howard had structured the play flawlessly, his characters were beautifully drawn, and

Stuart had created an internal dynamic that resulted in an almost unbearable emotional intensity.

I quickly got my new general manager, Dick Seader, down to see it, and told him I was thinking of optioning it for Broadway. Deeply affected and still absorbing what he had just seen, Dick immediately said, "I'll tell you this: If you don't, someone else will."

Howard and I were tight at the time, having gotten along incredibly well during "Dreamstuff," and he was delighted at the prospect. But he was using the workshop to try to land an agent, and my concern was that I had to insinuate myself as already in place as producer lest the new agent might want to shop it elsewhere.

The two agents who were most interested in Howard were Bret Adams, who ran a respected eponymous boutique agency, and Esther Sherman of the William Morris Agency. I knew Bret and had nothing against him, but I (perhaps naively) felt that the WMA imprimatur would provide more clout, and I recommended to Howard that he go with Esther. He did, and she became one of the very few people Howard never discarded as his career ascended. In her own way, she was also very supportive of our collaboration on "The Confirmation."

We knew we couldn't "sell" Stuart as the director of a new Broadway play, so I began shopping it to high profile directors. Arthur Penn was very interested in it, but he was tied up for the next 18 months. At that point in our lives, a year-and-a-half seemed like an eternity, so we didn't pursue it further. Instead, I got the script directly to Robert Moore, who basically had the same response, that he was quite taken with the play but his schedule was full to overflowing. And on down the line.

Our first choice for star was Jack Klugman. I got it to Klugman through my former stage manager – the wonderful Peter Lawrence – who had worked with him on the tour of "The Odd Couple." (I tried to avoid agents whenever I could as it was common knowledge they were more interested in placing clients in lucrative Hollywood work than a potentially long Broadway commitment.) But eventually Klugman called me to say he wasn't interested. So we moved on to our second choice, Herschel Bernardi, who was.

All of this took time – lots and lots of waiting time, which drove me crazy – and by that point Esther had convinced Howard and me to meet with her client Ken Frankel, who had won praise for his staging of Mark Medoff's off-Broadway hit, "When You Comin' Back, Red Ryder?" a few years earlier. Ken wasn't exactly what we had in mind when we started the search, but we wanted to get going, so we hired him.

I needed, of course, to find a way to come up with the Broadway capitalization of $280,000. I quickly learned that it was harder to raise money for a straight play than a musical because there's no score to play for potential investors at backers' auditions. It was then that the "Dreamstuff" lighting designer introduced me to a supposedly wealthy business tycoon from Florida who was looking for a show to finance. He went by the name "Dig."

"Dig" didn't want to be involved in the line producing, so Ken, Howard, and I immediately began a series of auditions to cast the rest of the roles, the most crucial of which was the female lead to (essentially) play Howard's mother. Finding the right actress proved more difficult than we had anticipated, so after an exhaustive search in New York, we flew to Los Angeles to hold more auditions there. The date was July 14, 1977. It's easy to be precise about this because we left New York City in the middle of the infamous blackout. We were more than a little surprised that taxis were on the streets and planes were taking off on schedule, so we were successfully able to make our escape.

Once in LaLaLand, we settled into our rooms in an old-style-Hollywood hotel on Sunset Strip that made us feel as if we had landed in Nathanael West's *Day of the Locust*. Before we began our auditions, Howard called a contact he had at Disney whom he had dealt with in his "day job" as an editor at Grosset and Dunlap, and she arranged for us to tour the studio.

When we arrived at the Disney lot, little did I – or he – have any remote notion of the historic role he would play less than two decades later in returning the studio's animation department to its former glory.

We stopped a fresh-faced, ultra-clean-cut young woman to ask directions to the office of Howard's contact. She smiled a plastered-on Disney smile and told us, earnestly and without a hint that there was anything unusual in what she was saying, to "walk down here and take a left on Mickey Avenue, then in a bit you'll come to Dopey Drive. Take a right at Dopey Drive, and the building will be on your left."

It was hard to keep from laughing as I looked at Howard, whose expression conveyed that he was experiencing his first encounter with an interplanetary lifeform.

Back in the real world (relatively speaking) of Los Angeles, we began holding auditions in the Masonic Temple on Hollywood Boulevard. Toward the end of our second and final day, an actress was in the middle of her audition when suddenly the door burst open and a yapping little dog ran in. A few seconds later, the actress Zohra Lampert, who was scheduled next, ran in after it.

The auditioning actress stopped and stared. As the cliché goes, if looks could kill. That actress no doubt became more apoplectic when she would later learn we hired Zohra. This decision raised some eyebrows among people I knew in the business based on her past stage experiences, but Ken was confident he could handle her. She had a shaky reputation in terms of being easy to work with, but she had two Tony nominations and an Emmy Award to her credit. Ken and Howard loved her reading and unhesitatingly wanted her. I felt the magic in her audition as well but did worry that she was slightly off-type for the role. She was represented by the same

ICM agents who handled Herschel, so the contract process went smoothly.

With star and director in place, Dick Seader found an opportunity for a pre-Broadway run-up that is common now but was actually new at the time (although similar in concept to what we had done with "Dreamstuff" on a smaller scale): take it through regional theaters in a partnership with a non-profit. McCarter Theatre Center in Princeton had an arrangement with the Annenberg Center in Philadelphia whereby a show would play three weeks on subscription in Princeton followed by two on subscription in Philly. It sounded perfect, and we struck a deal with McCarter's managing director at the time, Ed Martenson. We would use part of our capitalization to supplement McCarter's costs as well as the weekly differential between their favored nations regional theatre contract and what Herschel's first-class contract called for him to receive.

In the early going, "Dig" met me dollar for dollar in meeting preliminary costs. And he appeared one day with over $11,000 in "front money" from an investor. No reason not to trust.

Until there was. With the show fully cast and only weeks away from production, the funds he had assured us would be there didn't show up. He said there was a day's delay, but not to worry. Then another day, and another, until it became clear the money was a figment of his imagination. What made me delay in accepting the truth he was a fraud was the fact that he had already expended significant sums of his own money, and why would he do that if he were living a lie?

One late afternoon as we were approaching crunch time, he called to rant that the Park Avenue woman he had recently started courting had been playing games with him and that he had just listened to her on the phone screaming all sorts of things about other commitments she had and bad-mouthing our budget and Broadway and anything else she could think of.

I hung up, knowing we were dead in the water and not knowing where to turn.

Then, suddenly, my phone rang.

An unfamiliar female voice on the other end said, "Everything he said to you was a lie! I heard every word!"

It seemed that Dig's phone, which had three-way-calling, hadn't disconnected from the Park Avenue woman before he called me. So she listened. And then looked me up in the phonebook.

This was surreal. But things she said rang true. She made clear that she would indeed be interested, but only if Dig was out of the picture entirely. She and I agreed to meet the next day.

I realized that Dig would probably be relieved to be given a gracious way to get off the hook, and I was in a position where I had no choice. One route looked like a dead end, whereas the other offered promise. It would also offer the side benefit of resolving a problem with Herschel, who had despised Dig from a comment he had made one day when he saw Herschel with a cigar in his mouth. "I see you're smokin' Joe Louis' finger," Dig had said, and Herschel had rightly taken offense and not forgotten.

The next day this mystery woman and I met, along with a young fellow – a local kid's tv show host – she brought along with her. I never fully understood the relationship between them, but he became part of the package with a lesser financial role. We reached a deal in less than an hour. Because we were about to begin rehearsals, there was no choice but for each of us to put up half of the immediate $75,000 we needed to get through Philadelphia, with the remainder of what was still needed to meet the full capitalization to be raised as we went. I rationalized that if the play was a good as I thought it was, having it on stage would make it easier to attract the funds; if not, I could limit my losses to under $50,000, which would be painful but not crippling. The bank accounts would be in both our names, and two signatures would be required for all debit transactions. At first I thought of this as mutual protection since we didn't know each other.

Oh yeah, one other thing. She announced to me that she was an "actress, Stephen," although she had no credits other than a few acting classes, and I suspected no talent. But she wanted to audition to understudy for the female lead when we reached the point of addressing that, while at the same time she insisted she didn't want to be accorded any favoritism. I was worried and embarrassed about how to present this prospect to Herschel (when I eventually told him, he just laughed), but that was a problem for another day way down the line. "Park Avenue Ladies" – bored middle-aged women of comfortable means who wanted to be producers (not just investors) but in most cases were no more than crazed dilettantes – had become a burgeoning presence in the business by virtue of their checkbooks, and here I was in bed with one. I kept telling myself, show business, like politics, makes strange…oh, God.

So with all in order, rehearsals began in what were, at the time, one of the classier Broadway rehearsal venues (trust me, some of them back then were pretty scuzzy). The first week of rehearsals went smoothly, as is most often the case while the director and cast get to know each other and find a working dynamic. If problems are to arise, it's usually in the second week that they surface. And in our case, they came in the form of Ken Frankel expressing his frustrations with our lead actress.

At first, I discounted this given Ken's gruff personality that took some getting used to (I'm not sure I ever did). But his complaints to me became more frequent. And then Howard began expressing his concerns to me as well. When I'd ask Herschel for his thoughts, he'd just look at me and change the subject.

Finally, Ken held the first rough run-through of the show, and I immediately saw the legitimacy of their concerns. None – I mean, none – of the magic we saw in Zohra's approach to the role back in her Los Angeles audition was remotely evident. We knew we weren't crazy; all three of us had seen it, and our decision to hire her on the basis of it had been immediate and unanimous.

Ken and Howard kept trying to tap into it again, to convey what we had seen in her that we liked so much, but each subsequent run-through showed no signs of progress. And now Ken was saying things like "When we fire her, I want to be the one to do it!"

Of course, when that time came, as was inevitable, Ken was nowhere to be found and the task fell to me. Herschel was now in favor of this move; fortunately, he had told this to their mutual agent as well, of course with the understanding that she would be discreet in what she said to Zohra.

Our biggest problem was that time was not on our side. We were to begin performances in Princeton in about ten days, and the McCarter schedule was immovable. So I got a few tips on what to say from Dick Seader, who had experience in firing people from a show. He then lightheartedly told me, "Just don't end up moving in with her."

He went on to explain that apparently when Charles Grodin, who was directing a comedy called "Lovers and Other Strangers" on Broadway back in 1968, went to Zohra's apartment to fire her during rehearsals, the sparks of romance were kindled and she remained hired.

After phoning her agent to let her know what I was doing, I called Zohra and asked to meet with her. She said she'd rather not, that she was busy studying her lines. My heart broke, but I had to tell her that this wasn't working, and I did. It was all quiet and civilized, but not a pleasant message to have to give to a nice lady.

We obviously had to find her replacement quickly, and Ken and Howard remembered an actress they had both liked during auditions. In L.A. We all wanted her to read with Herschel before committing to her, so I flew her to New York on less than a day's notice with her suitcases packed for an extended stay in case she was hired.

But she wasn't. The chemistry didn't work. Another few grand down the drain. So immediately on to actresses in New York. It came down to two, one who was dead-on in terms of type, and one who wasn't. We went with Marilyn Chris, the one who wasn't. And we didn't regret it. Marilyn miraculously managed to put together a stage-worthy performance in the five days she had, and it got better and better as time went on. It didn't take her long to nail the exquisite final speech Howard had written for her character to deliver to her broken husband, trying desperately to give him a reason to go on, but with each word unknowingly driving a stake deeper into him.

We transitioned to McCarter and saw the finished set for the first time. I had been concerned when the designer, Marjorie Kellogg, had initially shown us the model, but Ken and Howard wanted to go with it, so we did. I thought that putting the entire house on stage would work against the sense of claustrophobia that Stuart White had so effectively captured in the Circle workshop, but Ken and Marjorie thought exactly the opposite and I felt I had no choice but to defer to them and Howard. When artists are in alignment and feel strongly about a creative decision, the producer has little he can do but to go along (unless it's financially impractical, of course), even when he disagrees with them, unless he wants to court chaos. The only power he truly has is to close the show (or formally withdraw if he has partners), which is almost always a totally counter-intuitive option.

Upon seeing the set fully realized, though, I felt my instincts had been correct, and, to this day, I consider it one of the principal problems with the production. When things were bleakest, I sometimes wondered whether, when we closed, I could put a fourth wall on it and move in.

My (God-help-me!) producing partner and I continued looking to finish raising the full capitalization, and, with performances going well if not great, some respectable, though far-from-ecstatic reviews began to appear along with a handful of mildly negative ones. The one exception to this was an out-and-out rave in the

Jersey section of the *New York Daily News*, which predicted that the play would move on to Broadway for a long run. While this review did wonders for company morale, it created another headache for us: union warnings that the set at McCarter had not been built in a union shop. We were already aware of this, but it being red-flagged by the powers-that-be at Local One, the stagehands union, only meant that we'd have to spend even more than we had anticipated to get an IATSE stamp on it when the time came.

Meanwhile, Howard was beginning to have issues with Herschel's performance. I was in the McCarter lobby one day during a performance when Howard came storming out of the theatre shouting, "I have to rewrite this play because the man can't act it!" This was vintage Howard.

For the most part while we were in Princeton, I left Howard alone to work creatively with Ken, but our contract with McCarter stipulated that following one matinee performance he had to participate in an "audience talkback" session moderated by McCarter's Artistic Director at the time, Michael Kahn. Howard vehemently refused. I told him he had no choice.

"I'm in the middle of rewrites and the last thing I need is to have my mind clouded by a lot of people who don't know anything about writing telling me what's wrong with my play!" he fumed.

But he finally realized he had to acquiesce. So when the moment came and he and Kahn were ready to start, Kahn asked him if he had any opening comments to make.

Howard stood up and, in a low voice, addressed the audience. "I have only one thing to say. I wrote this play for my father, who died." And he stoically sat back down.

I stood in the rear of the theatre and marveled at his ingenuity. The result was that not a single audience member brought up anything of a remotely critical nature, and it was probably the shortest post-performance discussion on record. Howard almost always knew how to get his way.

As we entered our third and final week in Princeton, everything began to get more intense, except, to my mind most crucially, the drama on stage. I've always been able to be very objective about how a show of mine is working (with one exception, which we'll get to later), and, while I realized that the production we had mounted was first-rate in every regard, it was coming off as being interesting but not dynamic, as it had been in the Circle workshop. I drove Dennis Green, my treasured "Dreamstuff" lyricist, down from New York to see it one night since he had also seen the workshop, and I recall afterwards, upon our return to the city, us sitting in my car for a long time outside his apartment building discussing how specifically I could constructively address this missing dynamic with Howard and Ken. The problem was that it defied specificity; it wasn't a case of cutting a scene here, adding one there. Everything worked dramatically, just not impactfully enough. I balanced this with the realization that audiences wouldn't have the Circle workshop to compare it to as we did.

But good news came that week. The Park Avenue Lady and her kids' show host sidekick showed up at McCarter after a performance one night carrying with them a signed check and Limited Partnership Agreement for $78,400 from a high-rolling investor in Philadelphia. This was essentially the final piece of the capitalization that would ensure our continuation beyond Philly to Broadway. Rarely have I experienced such relief.

Of course, though, there was another problem. We were in a holding pattern for a Broadway theatre because none were available. Dick Seader and I had met with Bernie Jacobs in his Shubert office about a month before rehearsals began and, for the first time in years, there was a booking crunch. We'd have to wait for a few of the fall shows to close. Nederlander likewise was jam-packed. Once we were in performances, Dick suggested we invite David Cogan, the owner of the independently owned Biltmore Theatre on West 47th Street, to come see it since he was actually the one theatre owner who was actively looking for a booking.

Dick called me in Princeton the morning after Cogan came. For some reason that neither of us understood – and certainly weren't prepared for – the play had offended Cogan. He told Dick that he'd rather keep his theatre dark than to book this play into it.

What? Not to like it was one thing, but to be offended by it to such a degree? We were mystified and disappointed, but we chalked it up as a freak response and moved on. I didn't even tell Howard, Ken, or Herschel about the harshness of Cogan's opinion because I didn't want to convey information that could needlessly hurt them.

I don't think I told the Park Avenue Lady either, mostly because she was becoming more and more impossible to deal with, questioning legitimate costs that had been incurred prior to her involvement, and not listening to what any of the professionals around her were saying. She was also focused on her upcoming understudy audition and "studying" for it. When Ken scheduled the auditions for one day toward the end of the Princeton run, I called and told her that her time to shine had come.

She went berserk, screaming, "I can't DO it tomorrow, Stephen! I'm having my period!"

As we arrived in Philly to start our two-week engagement at the Annenberg Center, much more devastating news than her period greeted us. The Utah bank that the check for $78,400 had been drawn on had refused to honor it. It had been returned to our bank, and was now in the hands of our attorney, Jeremy Nussbaum.

Jeremy sought to get to the bottom of the problem, especially since it didn't seem to be a case of insufficient funds in the account. The Park Avenue Lady couldn't get any answers from the investor either. But he had signed the papers and was legally obligated.

I knew we had two problems in pursuing this legally, though, despite having the grounds to do so. First, there was no time. The law is often rendered ineffective once a production gets underway. We were incurring costs daily, and the law usually takes an eternity to resolve a case.

Second, based upon what I had heard of the investor, I didn't want my stay in Philly to include a visit to the bottom of the Schuylkill River.

It was still possible that Jeremy could get the Utah bank to honor the check and legal commitment, but not being able to count on that, we knew we had to desperately look for new sources. We hoped our quest would be bolstered by the Philadelphia reviews.

The morning after our official opening, Dick, my ever-loyal associate Howard Rogut, and I drove to pick up the reviews in the lobbies of the newspaper buildings. First up was *The Philadelphia Inquirer*, and its respected critic, William Collins, while not writing a rave by any means, gave us hope.

Although qualifying his praise, Collins called Howard "clearly gifted" and said, "Written with a moral passion that can't help but make us think of Arthur Miller, 'The Confirmation' finds the stuff of an American tragedy in our suburban wastelands."

Our spirits were buoyed as we continued driving over to the *Philadelphia Daily News*.

And then they were shattered. David Cogan, it turned out, was not alone in being offended.

"Ashman's 'Confirmation' Is an Insult" was the headline on *Daily News* critic Jonathan Takiff's review. This wasn't a case of a headline writer making it up; it came from the final words of Takiff's review, which read "insulting to all Jews."

Having dismissed Howard from the get-go as a "cynical young playwright," rather than see the play as an "American tragedy" as Collins did, he couldn't get beyond the contempt he felt at the depiction of the moral decay and dashed dreams within a lower-middle class Jewish family. "The conclusions are downright insulting to the very audience who'll hear them people (sic) who've worked hard to buy theater tickets and nice clothes and to better their lot in general," Takiff argued.

Maybe I had been wrong. The production did have a strong dynamic. Just not the one we wanted or ever saw coming. Suddenly we became known as "that anti-Semitic play," despite it having been written by a Jew, directed by a Jew, and starring Tevye himself.

This had to have been a crushing blow for Howard to read such a condemnation when he had never intended for his words to have that effect. For the most part, he kept to himself at this point, except for one night, unbeknownst to me, he brought his partner and original director, Stuart White, down to Philly for a private meeting with Herschel.

What had prompted this, I think, was that Ken was now wavering in his feelings about the play. As the fallout from the Takiff review took on a life of its own around us, Ken said to me, "I was thinking, I don't know how I'd feel about my family seeing this play." What? He had never even hinted at that before.

Dick began analyzing all the reviews we had received, and he found an interesting pattern: the positive ones had been written by non-Jews while the negative ones had been penned by Jews. (Some of the latter touched on Semitic concerns, but not to anywhere near the extent Takiff's did.) He looked ahead to New York and noted that none of the major critics were Jewish. But the audience predominantly was, and one of the major theatre party agents had suddenly begun expressing her discomfort with promoting us to her usual groups.

One person who wasn't deterred by any of this was the producer Alex Cohen, who at the time was in charge of booking a subscription series at the Mechanic Theatre in Baltimore. Apparently having had a show drop out, he offered us a three-week engagement there, which would perfectly dovetail with our closing in

Philadelphia and would give us an ideal first-class venue in Howard Ashman's hometown prior to Broadway, as well as provide us with the time we needed for a New York theatre to become available. The subscription would insulate us from losses during the run, but we needed to close out the capitalization to get there.

Jerry Nussbaum was having little success getting any positive resolution to the matter of the $78,400 check he had sitting in his desk drawer, and the Park Avenue Lady had gone into full retreat mode, thinking the answer at this point was for her to say "no" to everything, even established commitments. Actually, her refusal to add her signature to mine on per diem checks for the Philly run led to the only lighthearted memory of this time.

Already late distributing them, we were facing a bit of a crisis with Ken and our actors. Actors' Equity was telling the cast not to perform that evening if they didn't receive them. I sent Howard Rogut to her New York apartment to get her to sign the checks no matter how he had to convince her. He called me from her apartment, exasperated. He told me she was taking a bath and was refusing to come out of the bathroom.

"Finally we get a break!" I told him. "Go in there and don't let her out of the tub until she signs them!"

To his everlasting credit, that's exactly what he did. According to Howard, she screamed about calling her lawyer, but since she didn't have a phone in the bathroom, she finally had to sign. Howard beat it back to Philly, we distributed the checks, and the show went on that night.

But by this time, it was becoming obvious that we were out of options. The firestorm set off by the Takiff review and the bad check had spelled our doom. I wasn't able to find any replacement funds, particularly with the anti-Semitic charges hovering around us. I think it was Ken who finally concluded that Jews weren't comfortable watching their dirty laundry being laundered in front of the goyim. It was as intelligent an analysis as anyone had.

One night in our final week at the Annenberg, about 10 minutes after the performance ended, I came up to the lobby from the downstairs dressing room area and saw about 20 audience members surrounding Herschel and having an animated but totally civilized dialogue about what they had just seen. I thought, man, this is why I got into theatre, and we're closing on Sunday.

Truth is, I still had enough money to round out the capitalization myself without going into personal debt. But if I lost it, I'd be scraping bottom. So it was now up to me whether we proceeded on to Baltimore, and then to Broadway.

I gave it serious thought. It was my nature to roll the dice, but also to assess the odds. I didn't want to shut down the production here in Philly after all the work we had put in. But we had already lost the sales support of at least one of Broadway's "theatre party ladies." A Broadway theatre owner and a Philadelphia critic had already said they were offended by the play's content and had deemed it anti-Semitic. And, while this was a first-rate production in every way, Frankel's staging of it lacked the dynamic that Stuart White had created in the workshop. In the end, I simply couldn't justify the production's very uncertain future as being worth the enormous personal risk I'd be taking.

In one of the toughest phone calls I ever had to make, I called Roy Somlyo, Alex Cohen's general manager, and told him we had to pass on the Mechanic.

The Sunday before we opened in Philly, a lengthy interview with Howard had appeared in the *Inquirer*, under the headline "Here's a playwright who can do without big-time Broadway." It read, in part:

"Other people are looking toward Broadway, not me; I don't really care," said Ashman.

"I don't see Broadway as the big time," he said. "To me the 'big time' is having a first-rate cast, which I have, a very talented director, which I have, having all the technical elements in place and fully realized, which I think they are. And the opportunity to see my play on a stage and to work on it to make it as good as I can."

I didn't take all of Howard's quote at face value then and I don't now. But the part about him not needing Broadway very much rang true as the years went on. Sadly and perplexingly, Broadway never acted as if it needed him either, at least while he was alive.

Realizing Impossible Dreams

At the same time that Howard and I were out-of-town with "The Confirmation," another joint – and, in the long view, more significant – project we had embarked on the prior year was coming to fruition in New York.

It was a theatre company of our own.

I mean, why not? Isn't that what any ambitious, red-blooded New York producer and writer in their mid-20s would try to pull off?

The opportunity had presented itself to me one day soon after "Dreamstuff" had finished its run at the WPA. Harry Orzello, who with his partners, Dan Dietrich and Virginia Aquino, had founded the WPA in 1971 and run it for five years, called me to say that he had decided to exclusively pursue his acting career and that the WPA was folding. He wanted to assure me that the money they owed me in loans I had made to them above and beyond my initial "Dreamstuff" commitment would be reimbursed in the final accounting.

Without even stopping to think, I responded, "Forget the money. Why don't you let me have your theatre instead?" If I could be appointed Producing Director in his and Dan's place, I could try to make a go of it.

His board of directors had decided they didn't want to bear the responsibility of hiring a new regime, so I'd be able to start with a clean slate and put together my own board, maybe with two of them remaining as members for continuity. And what made it all viable was that the WPA had become an established annual recipient of grants from both the National Endowment for the Arts (NEA) and the New York State Council on the Arts (NYSCA).

Harry was intrigued, although I'd have to accept the fact that the theatre was losing its lease at 333 Bowery, and I'd have to find a new space. I saw no problem with that since I didn't enjoy dodging the winos on the block anyway.

I immediately called Howard and appointed him Artistic Director. There wasn't a moment's hesitation either in my asking or him accepting.

As Harry and I were finalizing the details of the transition with his board, Howard started lobbying me to make his partner, Stuart White, his co-Artistic Director. I kept telling him I didn't really know Stuart, so Howard, in a series of phone calls, kept telling me how wonderful a talent he was. I had seen Stuart's staging of "The Confirmation," and had obviously been impressed, but that was my only point of reference.

Finally, on one of his lobbying calls, I said, "You know, Howard, can't Stuart speak for himself?"

Howard paused, then answered that I was right. Stuart called me. We met over Sunday brunch, just the two of us, and I was totally won over. There'd now be three of us.

Soon there'd be a fourth. They were good friends with a young guy named Kyle Renick, who was toiling as a business subordinate at Wynn Handman's American Place Theatre on West 46th Street and was anxious to find a new opportunity. He had experience writing grants and interacting with the NEA and NYSCA. I met Kyle and he became our Managing Director.

One of the first things we wanted to do was change the name of the theatre. WPA stood for Workshop of the Players Art, but the acronym had already been made famous by the Roosevelt-era Works Project Administration back in the 1930s. And while we wanted the American experience and culture to be our artistic focus, we didn't want our name to be confused in the public consciousness with a well-known Depression-era initiative.

I had brought Jeremy Nussbaum into the mix as our attorney, and he put a quick end to that desire of ours. His take was that if we changed the theatre's name, we'd lose our funding as well as our already established 501(c)(3) status as a recognized not-for-profit organization. So we kept it.

We started meeting regularly and determined that the entire upcoming 1976-77 season would be devoted to organization and to finding and moving into a new space. This meant Howard, Stuart, and Kyle would have to keep their day jobs for at least another year.

The three of them also knew a young and ambitious designer named Edward "Hawk" Gianfrancesco, who had building skills as well. He eagerly hopped aboard our dream train and began scouting available spaces to lease.

I was spending much more money than I should have been, especially with "The Confirmation" needing injections of preliminary cash as well. I also felt compelled to help Howard out financially to the extent I could, both through loans and, at one point, the commission of a treatment for a musical idea he had, as he and Stuart were truly struggling. In one of the many conversations he and I had in theatre stairwells during "The Confirmation," I eventually waived repayment of about half of the interest-free loan amounts I had made to him over the course of the preceding year.

At about the same time that Hawk found a second-floor loft space on Fifth Avenue at 19th Street, which he said he could convert into a theatre, we received bad news from Jeremy. Both the NEA and NYSCA had determined that, due to the extent of the WPA's administrative overhaul, they were considering us a new entity and wouldn't grant us any funding until the then-standard two-year waiting period for any new theatre had passed.

45

So now we had no state or federal money we could count on… the anticipation of which was the impetus to embark on this endeavor in the first place.

We met in my Tudor City apartment and sulked for hours. And then we did the only logical, acceptable thing we could think of: We decided to forge ahead regardless.

As we proceeded, it was on a true wing and a prayer, propelled only by our determination and belief in ourselves. To this day, I don't know how we scraped together all the money we needed; I recall that a lot was done on credit and everyone's personal pleas for small donations, and a lot was done by calling in favors everywhere, in addition, of course, to what I provided at increasingly regular intervals.

Stuart shared with the rest of us his strong desire to direct a revival of Edward Albee's adaptation of Carson McCullers' novella, *Ballad of the Sad Café*, as our inaugural production in the fall of 1977. The play had originally been produced on Broadway in 1963, but had only managed to run a few months despite a much-heralded star turn by Colleen Dewhurst. Stuart, though, was convinced he knew how to make it work in our intimate 100-seat space.

We were all fine with that, assuming Albee would give his blessing. It was a long shot, but Howard was able to connect with Albee through their mutual agent, Esther Sherman, and, once in contact, Stuart sold Albee on his vision. He decided to trust us.

By the time Hawk finished constructing the theatre space, we had decided that only Kyle really needed a separate office since he'd be there the most, and the rest of us could use the large bullpen space when we were there. Once Hawk put the wooden walls up to create that office, along with a box office in what became the lobby, activity began to be centered at this, our new address: 138 Fifth Avenue.

As active production work on "Ballad" began, Howard and I were devoting the bulk of our time and efforts to "The Confirmation." Kyle would call me whenever he needed my input or if there was an urgent need for more funds, and, as summer turned into fall, I would often leave checks with my doorman for either him or Stuart to pick up if I couldn't make it down to the theatre. Since Howard lived with Stuart, his lines of communication were easier.

Howard and I missed the entire rehearsal period of "Ballad," and, unless Howard snuck back from Princeton without my knowing it, neither of us even made it to the opening night of our new theatre. What I find amazing in retrospect is that at no time before "The Confirmation" began rehearsals did either Howard or I ever broach to the other the idea that it might make more sense to shut down the "Broadway Express" we were on and to regroup, mounting his play as part of our first WPA season instead, with Stuart directing. I look back on this as a major mistake on both our parts.

Once I accepted the sad reality that there was nothing more I could do to reverse the fate of "The Confirmation," I drove up from Philly to finally see our inaugural production. By then, "Ballad" was selling out and critics were throwing bouquets, most significantly the usually non-adjectival Mel Gussow in the *Times*. His was the type of review producers dream of, reading, in part, "This is, in all senses, an act of recovery. The play occupies a secure place in Mr. Albee's body of work. The production is harmonious in every detail. And the WPA's return in its handsome new headquarters is a notable event for Off Off Broadway."

Writing that "the entire production has an air of authority and authenticity," he went on to cite the dirt that Hawk had brought in to cover the stage floor: "...not just a patina of silt, but cartloads of real earth, packed down so that there is a crusty realistic surface." The play's famous final scene, a brutal wrestling match between the lead character whom Gussow described as a "man-mountain of a woman" and her estranged husband, with an unexpected intervention by her dwarf cousin, was singled out in the review's final paragraph: "The scene is played with ferocious conviction – dust flying, coating the combatants, and a few of the spectators. The fight becomes a passionate, ritualistic battle for identity, control, and survival."

Stuart had again created the intensity that I had found to be missing in "The Confirmation" without him. And he had instantly established our credentials as a theatre company to be respected.

Following the performance I attended, the extraordinarily talented lead actress, Kaiulani Lee, signaled to me with her finger that she wanted to talk to me. She pleaded with me to set the wheels in motion for an off-Broadway transfer. I knew that an intimate space was essential for Stuart's production to work – Gussow had even noted in his review that, "At the WPA, the play finds its natural, novella-size environment" – but I also knew from first-hand experience that making the commercial economics work for a large cast show in a small theatre would be next to impossible. And, with "The Confirmation" in its death throes, I didn't have the stomach or the wallet for it at this moment. Kaiulani kept lobbying and pleading with me, though. The next day she called me to apologize for being so brazen, and I told her to never say she was sorry for expressing passion for her work.

Shortly after the WPA run ended, Kyle received calls from both the NEA and NYSCA. Representatives from each had seen the production, and both organizations had decided to restore our funding right away. We now had a little financial breathing room, although not enough to pay salaries to ourselves, which wouldn't happen for another several years when, finally, Kyle was able to draw a whopping $25,000 a year for his full-time commitment. From early on, I considered him the backbone of the operation; he always kept the WPA as his sole focus, while Howard and I were off pursuing other projects and positions. How Kyle ever survived, living and paying rent in New York City, for all the years he did has always been a mystery to me, but I do know the WPA only survived for as long as it did because of his dedication to it.

For me personally, back in the fall of 1977, it was just nice to have a success and a home to come back to.

Making Our Mark

I may have missed the loading in of all the dirt for "Sad Café," but I sure as hell was there for its removal. I know because I helped with it. As we all did. Even John E. Allen, the dwarf actor who had played Cousin Lymon in the production (why he was there, I don't know, but he was).

There was actually a nice communal feeling in the air that November day, working and having lunch at the local deli with colleagues who had banded together against all odds and whose first trip to the plate had been a home run. The dirt was bountiful though – definitely, as Mel Gussow had said, "not just a patina of silt," which had already become a phrase we all adopted to tease Hawk about his attention to detail.

With the dirt gone, it was on to the second production of the inaugural season. Even though it didn't fit neatly into our stated artistic mission, Howard and Stuart had become intrigued with an unusual piece of work that was hard to define but was ultimately labeled "an entertainment with music," based on the macabre stories and spidery drawings of Edward Gorey. The timing was propitious given that the highly anticipated Gorey-designed production of "Dracula," starring Frank Langella, was opening on Broadway that fall.

"Gorey Stories" was a much less extravagant enterprise. It had been created and performed at the University of Kentucky three years earlier but was still in need of development. We brought Tony Tanner in to work with the author, Stephen Currens, and his composer, David Aldrich. Tanner's sensibility seemed perfect for what the *Times* would call these "little Victorian melodramas, cliff-hanging Gothic tales of malfeasance, mischief, and pranks of fate."

With a first-rate cast of character actors that included veteran performers such as Liz Sheridan and Gemze de Lappe, Tanner began rehearsals, but, when he got to the point of stringing all the playlets together, he realized he had a dilemma. Sitting in the office bullpen one day, having appeared deep in thought while slowly twirling a yardstick, he unexpectedly drew our attention by casually announcing, "My darlings, we have a problem. We have no second act."

He didn't mean there were second act problems; he literally meant there was no second act. Once it was on its feet, the existing material ran all of 45 minutes, hardly a full or satisfying evening of theatre. Rather than panic, he and Currens quickly and quietly concocted a second act out of other Gorey material that they wove into an original conceit.

To be sure, it was a mission of creative desperation, and while we saw the imperfections in their efforts, we still thought we had a nice little show that we could get by with and then move on.

Much to our surprise, the critics and audiences disagreed with our internal assessment when we opened in early December. It was hats-in-the-air time. Gussow in the *Times* led the way, calling the show "a merrily sinister musical collage," and ending his rave review by saying "It is a show with wit, economy, and malice. In other words, the evening is etched in Gorey. To paraphrase [one of the Gorey stories] 'The Wuggly Ump,' 'Sing tirraloo, sing tirralay – for the WPA.'"

Commercial producers began descending upon us about moving the show, but the main impetus came from super-agent Sam Cohn at ICM who wanted us to schedule an extra performance for celebrities and heavy hitters he wanted to personally invite. ICM would even pay us $600 for the extra costs we would incur in arranging that. When the night of Cohn's performance arrived, a "who's who" of entertainment crossed the threshold of our theatre's humble home, which, lest I forget to mention, had a "massage parlor" on the floor above it.

Despite all of this excitement, we remained skeptical of the show's commercial prospects, but also felt that if it had a chance for success it would be off-Broadway, not on. Cohn, though, pushed instead for a small Broadway house, and a team of producers led by Terry Alan Kramer and Harry Rigby mounted it at the Booth Theatre the following October, with mostly the same cast but with Gorey himself designing the sets. It opened – and closed – on October 30, 1978, known in contemporary American culture, appropriately enough, as Mischief Night. Our initial instincts about its limited prospects had ultimately been proven to be on target.

What I remember most vividly about the show's WPA run was greeting Gorey when he entered the theatre, wearing a floor-length fur coat and looking every bit the eccentric personality he was, at the final performance just before Christmas.

"Merry Christmas, Mr. Gorey!" I intoned cheerfully.

He looked at me aghast and shivered while exclaiming in horror, "Christmas!"

The remainder of that first season was respectable but less noteworthy, starting with a new play called "If You Can't Sing, They'll Make You Dance," written and directed by Phillip Hayes Dean, a notable African American playwright of the time, that both critics and audiences pretty much correctly dismissed as a minor and flawed work by this respected yet somewhat controversial artist.

March brought with it a new comedy that I personally loved, written by Elia Kazan's son, Nick, and bearing the unlikely title, "April 2, 1979: The Day the Blanchardville, North Carolina Political Action and Poker Club Got the Bomb." It focused on a group of rednecks, one of whom was an auto mechanic who had made an atomic bomb that they thought they could use as leverage to have their dreams fulfilled. It was cast with stellar character actors, including Dann Florek, who went on to "Law and Order" fame, and audiences enjoyed it as the ludicrous lark it was intended to be. Critics were less enthusiastic, but the *Times* acknowledged that "In this, his first play produced in New York, Mr. Kazan would seem to have a considerable comic arsenal at his command."

The season bookended "Sad Café" with another production that Stuart directed based on the work of a Southern author, Reynolds Price, who had adapted his own 1962 novel, *A Long and Happy Life*, for the stage. Under the title "Early Dark," it was a gentle, lyrical mood piece about a young woman coming to terms with romance and how she wants her life to unfold in a small North Carolina town where a woman's role was defined by social limitations and expectations. The material was perfectly suited to Stuart's strengths as a director, and his production was exquisite. No one ever expected it to be more than a poignant evening, and on that level it succeeded with integrity to spare. It was never meant to be a blockbuster, but it brought our first season to a close with distinction.

My most lasting memories around its production have to do with two actresses in the cast (and, no, it's not what you're thinking!). The lead was played by a young woman who brought to the character a brooding depth that was magnetic. She won the critics' raves much more than the play did. During the rehearsal period, she had been down-to-earth and friendly. Once she became the critics' darling and was being sought after by major agents, she became aloof, as if the act of returning a simple "hello" was a chore for her. Let it be a lesson to artists everywhere that, subsequently, her career went nowhere.

My other memory is more personal. I hadn't been around too much during rehearsals, and I hadn't met many of the cast members. At performances, I'd sometimes enjoy the simple task of working box office, and on these nights, I'd be in lobby/office area during the performance. One of the young actresses in the show had to make her entrance from the rear of the house, so she'd be milling about in the same area. We started talking and I introduced myself.

"Oh, the father of the WPA," she said warmly.

Her simple recognition of that was meaningful to me. I had begun to wonder if anyone even knew of my true role in establishing this theatre company, although I was clearly listed as Producing Director. Part of this was my own fault because I have never been the sort of personality who engages in self-promotion. But a large part of it was that I had begun feeling like an odd man out in my own theatre. I felt incredible pride in the staff I had put together – in fact, I was convinced that Howard, Kyle, and Stuart were the best young talents in New York in their artistic and business capacities. Yet it had become increasingly apparent to me that, in structuring the new WPA, I had overlooked one vital thing: creating a fulfilling operational role for myself. Had any of the others had deficiencies of any sort, or needed course-correcting, that would have been different. But they were all so damned good at what they did that the only thing for me to responsibly be was a rubber stamp. I knew I didn't want to devote my energies solely to fund-raising, which I hated doing, but that was the only useful function I had left for myself.

I had also begun to feel a personal schism with Howard. In the year during which both the WPA and "The Confirmation" were in gestation, Howard, Stuart, and I had become quite close. They spent several evenings at my apartment playing Howard's favorite board game, *Risk*, with my crazy girlfriend and me. We'd talk on the phone at least daily. But "The Confirmation" had created an unspoken strain in Howard's and my relationship. Just as he had (I think wrongly) blamed Jim Nicola's staging for "Dreamstuff" not moving beyond the Bowery, now I felt he was silently (for the most part) making me the villain for "The Confirmation" not progressing beyond Philadelphia. (Personally, I don't think either of us could have foreseen or done anything more to try to overcome the insurmountable obstacles that the theatre gods threw in our path.)

I have always shown gratitude to, and remained friends with, everyone who has believed in, championed, and opened doors for me throughout my career. But I have learned through the years that many people aren't like that; they prefer to pretend they got to where they did by themselves. It's one of the sadnesses I've had in life, because in all cases they were people I genuinely liked and cared about, and Howard was the first of those.

During that first season, I actually became closer to Kyle, who was always friendly and self-effacing and would often seek out my advice. (How could you not like a guy whose favorite Disney character was Cruella de Vil?) I never doubted that his primary allegiance was to Howard, but he and I would remain allies over the next decade, with most of our conversations having to do with commercial transfer negotiations for several WPA productions. We didn't become good friends, but we liked and respected each other as fellow professionals. We never went out for drinks together, or socialized in any way, for the simple reason we had vastly different interests outside of theatre. I loved baseball, and Yankee Stadium had become my second home. Kyle was into opera and the "Village scene." If there's one thing that hurts me a bit it's that he followed Howard's lead and, in public writings and interviews through the years, wrote me out of the WPA's history. Somehow it magically became Howard, Stuart, and Kyle's creation – although it is curiously never explained *how* they landed in those positions or who had made it all possible.

Whatever.

Second Season

Over the summer of 1978, I continued wrestling with the personal paradox of having had my first major success in New York theatre in launching the WPA and my own day-to-day discontent in working there. Fortunately, I had one of the greatest and most dramatic Yankees baseball seasons ever to distract me.

Come that fall, though, back on lower Fifth, Stuart was at the plate again. We opened the season with his production of Lillian Hellman's unsuccessful 1936 play, "Days to Come," which was a family drama that focused on the impact of a labor dispute in a midwest brush factory and the havoc that came to be wrought by strikebreakers. With a major playwright like Albee singing our praises in the industry, it wasn't difficult to gain Hellman's trust.

There are two women of historic significance in American theatre whom I feel privileged to have had at least one passing experience with, and Hellman was one of them (the legendary agent Audrey Wood was the other). She didn't attend rehearsals, but did attend a performance, with one proviso: she didn't want the audience to know she was there. This meant having her arrive and sneaking her and her companion into the last row after the house lights went down. But when we flawlessly executed this strategy, the most amazing thing happened. The audience *sensed* her presence. Almost as one, they stood up, turned to her, and applauded. It appeared that she was touched, even if she hadn't wanted the attention.

We took her to Kyle's office during the two intermissions, where she asked if it could be arranged for her to speak to the cast after the performance.

With the actors literally assembled at her feet, and all of us packed into the small office, she thanked everyone, saying, "You've made me feel better about myself tonight." She went on to explain how she had always blamed herself for the play's failure 42 years prior, but that this production of it made her think that she had been too hard on herself.

As the cast hung on her every word, she went on to explain that she had always doubted herself too much and told a story about the opening night of one of her other plays. She related that she had watched the first act of the play from the back of the house, cringing at every word that came from the stage. When the first of the two intermissions finally came, she said she went up to the office where the producer (whom records show was Herman Shumlin) was relaxing.

"You've got to put an end to this embarrassment," she told him, and begged him to "bring the curtain down on it now" and apologize to the opening night audience and critics. She told him she'd reimburse him for all the losses he incurred. She pleaded with him and wouldn't let up.

She said he finally acknowledged her, calmly responding, "Sit down, Lillian, and have a drink."

The name of the play, she then revealed, was "Watch on the Rhine." It became one of her biggest successes.

She concluded her comments by telling the cast not to make the mistake she too often did. "Always believe in yourself," she told them.

Believing in myself had never been one of my problems; finding happiness in my work had been. I continued growing more distant from the day-to-day functions of the WPA and had begun searching for other projects to focus on. I was extremely proud of the success we had achieved at WPA against all odds and how quickly we had achieved it. But once it was up and running and had quickly garnered a level of recognition in the industry that most start-up theatre companies never get, I wanted new challenges where I would have a less passive role.

Sometimes the wisest thing a producer can do is simply not interfere with the artists he or she has hired. Years later, the actress Jodi Benson – one of the few interpreters of Howard's work whom he ever chose to work with twice – was quoted as saying about him, "If you were smart, you would just let him go and drive the train." By her criteria, I was smart...as, incredibly, was Jeff Katzenberg when Howard worked on the animated Disney films in subsequent years. I had a natural inclination to respect writers' desires, even when I wasn't convinced they were correct, but, in Howard's case, I never even disagreed with him on anything major, which maybe explains why he never threatened to "strangle" me, as he once did Katzenberg when the latter dared disagree with him on a song before backing down.

So feeling fairly useless unless I wanted to devote myself solely to fund-raising, which I didn't, and not enjoying the work environment, at some point fairly soon after "Days to Come," I resigned as Producing Director, ceding the title to Kyle. I did, though, remain involved through the theatre's board of directors, continuing to serve as its president for a while, although this was a relatively toothless advisory body.

The curious thing is that once I resigned from my official administrative role, I began to truly enjoy my affiliation with the WPA. Kyle and I would continue to speak regularly, and even frequently when we were dealing with commercial transfers. It wasn't that the WPA chose plays with the aim of having them move on to become Broadway or off-Broadway productions, it's just how it happened.

Of the four transfers that were to come in the next two years, it was only the first of those that I had nothing to do with negotiating: Howard's next project, a musical adaptation of Kurt Vonnegut's

1965 novel, *God Bless You, Mr. Rosewater*. I stayed far in the background on this from the get-go, partly due to my contentious prior dealings on "Wings" with Vonnegut's attorney, which would have surely stood in the way of the WPA acquiring even the limited stage rights it was granted, and partly to my still-strained relationship with Howard. But what happened with "Rosewater" was fascinating to observe.

Howard's original intention was to rekindle his collaboration with "Dreamstuff" lyricist Dennis Green and composer Marsha Malamet. Dennis immediately committed to the project, but Marsha was reluctant, preferring to pursue her "pop career," as she put it. Marsha seemed to often, and sadly, make the wrong career decisions, and her withdrawal from the team meant that a new composer needed to be found. Enter Alan Menken, whom Howard knew from their days in Lehman Engel's BMI Musical Theatre Workshop.

Not long into the creative process, Howard began moving toward more firmly defining himself as what in the film world is known as an *auteur*. He asked Dennis if he could share lyric-writing duties with him, and the ever-compliant Dennis agreed. But that arrangement soon morphed into Howard being *the* lyricist and Dennis being relegated to "Additional Lyrics By" status.

Howard also decided he'd become the director, establishing himself as a "triple threat" creator (book, lyrics, direction), which he also was on his two future stage musicals, "Little Shop of Horrors" and "Smile." He was nothing if not self-confident in his vision for a project and trusted almost no one to interpret it. Several years later, he and Marvin Hamlisch did have a lengthy (and taped) meeting with Bob Fosse about the latter possibly staging "Smile," but, despite Howard telling Fosse he'd give his right arm to have him direct it, Fosse didn't commit. (If he had, then that show might have succeeded, but I feel safe in predicting that Howard would have hated both him and the show by the time it opened on Broadway. As it was, his dislike of Hamlisch was inevitable.)

59

Going forward, if Howard was going to cede control to anyone, it would only be to a bona-fide A-list artist he respected and not some journeyman hack. When he and Menken later became involved with the Disney animated films that became instant classics and revived the Disney animation brand, he, of course, could no longer insert himself as director. But anyone who thinks that all he did for "The Little Mermaid" and "Beauty and the Beast" was write lyrics is delusional; the Ashman sensibility and structural acumen permeate both films, as well as the portions of "Aladdin" that were created before his death from AIDS in 1991.

But back to 1979. "Rosewater" was another success story at the WPA. It was a mostly low-key musical, savvy and literate. Mel Gussow in the *Times* called it "a jauntily misanthropic musical…a show with satiric bite and a devious mind."

It clearly had the potential to move to a commercial theatre. But the question was where?

For better or worse, this time it wasn't the WPA's problem. As part of the deal Howard and Kyle had made to get the rights to the novel, Vonnegut retained total control of the *commercial* stage rights.

Having been bestowed with that control, Vonnegut, who had fallen in love with the show, proceeded to give the rights to his daughter, Edie, as a birthday gift despite her having little or no theatre experience. (Pinch me.) But, fortunately, unlike the commercial producers on "Gorey Stories," neither she nor anyone else ever considered "Rosewater" a Broadway show. And since everyone – Howard most of all – wanted to move the production intact, with no cast changes or major rewrites, once the capitalization had been raised there was very little a producer could do to undermine its creative aesthetic. Except to put it in the wrong theatre.

The Entermedia was a mid-size theatre on 2nd Avenue in the East Village that felt larger than it was. Despite the fact that "Grease" and "Joseph and the Amazing Technicolor Dreamcoat" had opened there prior to moving to Broadway, it was perceived in the industry as an awkward venue, neither fish nor fowl, with an off-Broadway feel on the outside and a Broadway one inside. And this was where "Rosewater" landed.

In a 2016 Playbill interview, Kyle pointedly summed up the fatal impact the choice of the Entermedia had on the show: "It lost its intimacy, its sweetness, its innocence, and its Vonnegut authenticity, replaced by something bloated, loud, irritating and judgmental." And the critics weren't kind.

In that same Playbill interview, Edie Vonnegut acknowledged she should have waited for a smaller theatre to become available, even if that meant replacing some cast members. Howard had despised the Entermedia as a venue for this show, but he also didn't want to run the risk of having to re-cast any key roles by waiting. Such, though, are the choices that often must be made in commercial theatre.

And there's one overriding reality. Howard may have been the librettist, lyricist, and director, but the real power rested with Vonnegut…Kurt, not Edie. And Howard, Kyle, the WPA, and everyone else had no choice but to go along.

"Rosewater" opened at the Entermedia on October 14, 1979. It closed the Saturday after Thanksgiving.

My Dog Made Me Do It

If I had grown to feel superfluous at the WPA, except for my continuing role on the board, I hadn't hit upon what career move to make next. Eventually, my dog brought me the answer.

And, despite that, I continued to love and care for him until his death a dozen years later.

To explain, a precocious little boy had taken a liking to Fielding, my golden retriever, and had asked to walk him regularly. In due course, I met the boy's father, who was a director of industrial shows and various video projects, and we'd talk about the entertainment world. It came to pass that he was friends with a wealthy theatre lover and half-hearted entrepreneur who had earlier in life created and financed cheap horror films. They had an idea for a new venture and before long asked me to join them in it as a partner, and, God help me, I said yes.

As for their names, I don't want to speak ill of the dead, so let's just call them Sleaze and Dilettante. Someone later (and accurately) described Sleaze as the type of guy who wouldn't ask if he could "take you to lunch" but rather if he could "buy you a slice." Dilettante was a thoroughly nice guy who didn't really apply himself fully yet wanted to be more than the lightweight "wallet" he was generally viewed as.

As for the venture, it was called Theatre Vision International, or TVI for short. Ever hear of it? No? There's a reason for that.

The concept seemed pretty good at the time. It was to tape theatre productions of classics (in the public domain, to avoid "rights" issues and cost) at top regional theatres, by virtue of a three-way deal between TVI, the regional theatre, and the local PBS affiliate, which would supply the television production crew and equipment in exchange for initial broadcast rights. TVI and the regional theatre would then split the revenue from all subsequent licensing. Initial capital would come from Dilettante until there was a pilot product to show and sell to investors and buyers.

The taping was to be done with five cameras during regular live performances, which we felt was essential in order to capture the immediacy of a theatrical event.

The Proskauer firm, which represented Dilletante, forged an acceptable arrangement with Actors' Equity and AFTRA. The actors, on a favored nations basis, would get an amount equal to one week's pay, as well as residuals. Heck, this was "found" money for them.

Somehow, the tv department at William Morris joined the party, wanting to be our company's agent and doing what William Morris does best: waiting for clients to generate their own deals and then collecting its ten percent.

We decided to do a low-cost test production to see where the booby traps might be in the production process, and we made a deal with the PBS affiliate in Connecticut to shoot a nearby production of "Uncle Vanya," directed for the stage by Austin Pendleton, in an initial departure from his primary career as a character actor best known for playing nebbishes. Of course, Sleaze would helm the tv side of things in the control room.

The main thing we learned was that we had to handle the sound better; the clumping of feet was way too noticeable and distracting.

My primary memory of this time was sitting alone with Austin Pendleton, showing him the initial edit, and listening to any comments he had. Somehow we got to talking about his acting career, and, in all sincerity, he said, "I'm getting tired of always playing the nebbish [sniffle]. I don't know why I never get offered any leading man roles [sniffle]."

Okay, Austin.

So, having made and (for the most part) thrown out our first batch of pancakes, but having learned quite a bit from it, we moved on to our pilot project. It was summer, and there were two "classics" in rotating repertory at the Guthrie Theatre in Minneapolis. Dilettante knew its Managing Director at the time, Don Schoenbaum, and got an expression of, well, interested curiosity from him. So off we flew to Minnesota to see the shows.

One of them was a stunning production of "Camille" that had been directed by Garland Wright, whose best-known work was probably the 1976 off-Broadway play "Vanities," but who served as Associate Artistic Director of the Guthrie under Liviu Ciulei in the early '80s and then as Artistic Director from 1986-1995. We felt we had found our pilot project, and since Ciulei hadn't as yet arrived from Romania to assume his duties, Schoenbaum was the only person we had to convince.

The concept of having five cameras shooting from various angles in the aisles, while a regular theatre audience watched the play they had paid to see, frightened him. He didn't think it could be done without interfering with the audience's experience, but he agreed to let us try. There was a condition, though: If even one audience member complained, he would shut us down immediately. We agreed. The local PBS folk were already on board, so we were set to go.

We returned to New York and began preparations. First came a surprisingly difficult negotiation with the agent for the playwright who had adapted the original play. Then we had to make sure that the cast members agreed to the terms we were offering on a favored-nations basis. Richard Ramos, the Guthrie's Acting Artistic Director, called a cast meeting and reported back that the deal was acceptable to all.

After several weeks that I mostly spent on the phone with a Proskauer attorney (I can only imagine what Dilettante's bill from them was) finalizing contracts, we put those contracts under our arms and flew back to Minneapolis for the shoot.

Schoenbaum told me to use what would soon be Ciulei's office as my base of operations. And it was there that the bullshit started. No sooner had we arrived than I was handed a message from the Proskauer attorney to call him immediately. The adapter's agent had reneged on basic contractual terms we had settled on back in New York and had reverted to her original demands. Given that the adapter, a gentle lady named Barbara Field, was Playwright-in-Residence at the Guthrie, we had thought we'd just have her sign the contract upon our arrival since it had only been "finalized" a day before we left New York.

I called her into my office. She didn't know what to say; this tactic was obviously not of her doing, but her agent's. I told her that if she didn't sign the contract, we'd have to pack up and leave. She clearly didn't want that – especially since we were to pay her $10,000 upon the contract being executed -- but she was afraid to go against her agent, whom she said would stop representing her if she didn't do what she said. (The agent, by the way, had once worked for Audrey Wood, whom I later heard had fired her for being "too aggressive.")

Sitting in front of me, Field looked as if she was about to break down. Finally, she asked meekly that if she signed the contract would I help her land a new agent? Very moved by her situation, I said I would. She signed and we were still in business. And I immediately found her a more honorable agent going forward.

Next, I distributed the agreed-upon contracts to the cast members and met with each of them individually for the contracts to be signed. The actors seemed pleased and grateful to be part of this experiment and to make a few unexpected bucks for simply doing what they were already being paid to do. William Converse-Roberts, who played the male lead, was particularly delightful to deal with. I was a bit surprised by how nice a guy he was because, by the time I met with him, it had already come to my attention that he and his Camille, a now-deceased actress whose prickliness prompted us to give her the nickname "Snuggles," were not getting along. And, speaking of Snuggles, she quickly became the only cast member who hadn't signed a contract.

When I finally succeeded in getting her to come to my office, I immediately realized we had a problem. She tried to engage me in conversation about everything except putting her signature on paper. She was no amateur at flirting or espousing on how the production depended on her so maybe she deserved a tiny bit more remuneration than the rest. It was Diva Time, and she wanted to hold off signing until she could think about it for a few more hours.

She hadn't committed by the end of the day, and I was ready to confront her with an ultimatum. But, alas, Sleaze and Dilettante had fallen victim to her charms and decided we should take her to dinner in order to make her feel fully appreciated. I objected to playing into her diva routine, but they were determined.

So off we went to the top of the IDS Center. Fancy, expensive, and with a view of all of Minneapolis. But the first sign of what we were in for came on the elevator ride to the 57th floor when our leading lady curled up in a ball in the corner of the elevator, claiming claustrophobia. I knew then we were in trouble.

Once at the table, it became pretty much of a rambling monologue about her life and career, which Sleaze and Dilettante seemed charmed by, but which almost put me to sleep. She finally zeroed in on how, if her suggestions had been accepted, the production would have been oh so much better. This got her really wound up, and the intensity of her diatribe kept building and building until it was near its fever pitch.

"You know what the problem with this production is?" she asked, standing up.

"You know what the problem with this production is?" she repeated, louder. A few heads of diners nearby turned.

"I'll tell you the problem with this production!"

Even louder, almost screaming.

"THE PROBLEM WITH THIS PRODUCTION IS IT DOESN'T HAVE ENOUGH PUSSY JUICE!!!"

The whole restaurant went silent, as in the old E.F. Hutton commercial. She stormed off toward the ladies room as shocked stares came our way.

I felt conspicuous.

Even Sleaze and Dilettante were thrown.

Cut to the next morning. We handled it my way, I issued Snuggles an ultimatum, and the contract got signed.

So much for courting divas.

The rest of our mission went much smoother. We shot two performances with five cameramen positioned in aisles around the theatre, and not a single theatregoer complained. Don Schoenbaum was thrilled, and he offered to serve as a reference to his colleagues around the country whom we might approach for future shoots.

But, alas, there would be no future shoots. With far fewer potential outlets than exist today, there were no interested buyers for the product. It would be easy – and partially accurate – to blame William Morris' usual non-effort for this, but I think ultimately the hybrid form itself was problematic. We were able to improve the sound quality, but it still wasn't what television audiences were accustomed to. More significantly, though – and this has been shown in other tapings of stage productions as well – theatre promises an immediacy that television by nature can't capture on tape. The practice in recent years of doing live telecasts of productions comes closer to capturing that, but those are specifically staged for television. And they remain betrayed by the hybrid form.

The still-imperfect sound, though, did provide a moment of amusement during the editing process. There was a scene in the production that ended with Converse-Roberts carrying Snuggles offstage. Once they were off, we heard a loud thud that the sensitive microphones had picked up. We thought no, it couldn't be what we were thinking. So we checked the tape of the other recorded performance. Same thud in the same place.

I guess they *really* didn't like each other.

The Hits Just Keep On Coming

Meanwhile, back at the WPA, more commercial transfers were happening, which meant Kyle and I spent a lot of time talking on the phone, much of it trying to make sense of the nonsensical.

After "Rosewater," it wasn't long before the next one came our way, and this time it belonged on, and was destined for, Broadway. It was a courtroom drama by a writer/journalist named Tom Topor. I had known Tom since 1975 when he had interviewed me during rehearsals for "Wings" as part of a feature he was writing for the *New York Post* on young producers. His play, simply called "Nuts," opened at the WPA in late 1979, and a bidding war among bona fide Broadway producers started immediately.

With the play set in a courtroom in the psychiatric ward of Bellevue Hospital, Anne Twomey was giving a career-making performance in the lead role of a prostitute who had killed one of her clients in self-defense and was now fighting to prove her sanity so she could stand trial rather than remain committed. The unusual thing about the hysteria that was generated by several producers competing for the rights to move the play uptown was that it started almost immediately after the first performance and wasn't a matter of waiting for reviews.

It had always been our practice at WPA to try to follow writers' wishes as much as possible when it came to what producer or producing entity to entrust with a commercial move. Contractually, the decision was WPA's, but respect for writers and their preferences was always a priority for us. So the first step would usually be for a writer to meet with interested producers.

Topor's years as a journalist had made him street-wise when it came to Broadway, and he was always ready with a pithy comment about these meetings. But it didn't take him long to come to us with his choice. Universal Pictures had a division devoted to theatre, and Tom liked its deep corporate pockets. It currently had a long-running show – "The Best Little Whorehouse in Texas" – on Broadway, which had achieved longevity without being a mega-hit. Tom wanted that same type of insurance by choosing a production entity that had the wherewithal to keep "Nuts" running and promote it if it showed box office weakness during its run. Understandable.

The executive in charge of Universal's theatre division at the time was a woman named Stevie Phillips, known in the business for being tough, if not downright vicious. It was that lioness' den into which Kyle ventured.

The elements of a commercial rights deal – up-front fee, small percentage of gross receipts, and a percentage of net – were fairly standard; it was just the amounts that varied. And in the case of "Nuts," agreement on the numbers came easily. It was something else that didn't, something that had nothing to do with money but surprisingly turned out to be a huge sticking point. Since Universal was moving the WPA production intact, we wanted – and thought it fair – that the title page billing read "Universal Pictures presents the WPA Theatre Production of…"

Stevie Phillips categorically refused. Our billing would come at the bottom and would read "Originally produced by…" This implies it was a different production uptown, which it wasn't.

As a matter of principle, we said no. She offered more of Universal's money up front if we relented on this point. We refused, and when Kyle called to tell me of his conversation with Phillips, it became clear that the stories about the wrath she could display were not exaggerated.

This was getting insane. She kept upping her financial offer rather than giving in on a billing issue, although, as is often noted among producers, billing is the cheapest thing to give away.

She finally offered an amount that made no sense from Universal's end. Kyle and I both realized it had reached the point where refusing it would be irresponsible of us as directors of a not-for-profit organization.

Phillips was in Tokyo when Kyle called her to agree to her final offer. She accepted the deal but was seething. She told Kyle he could cram something "where the sun doesn't shine" and slammed the phone down.

A few months later, we discovered the reason she was so adamant on the billing point. The Broadway billing read "Stevie Phillips, in association with Universal Pictures..." Somehow she had gotten top billing for *herself* above Universal, her employer. She had unnecessarily spent thousands upon thousands of Universal's dollars, and tortured Kyle, simply to stroke her own ego. And the irony of this is that no one in the theatregoing public pays any attention to a producer's billing and professionals in the industry *know* who actually did what on a show.

Yet there was still one more "you're not going to believe this" moment ahead. As "Nuts" was winding down its WPA run, I ran into Topor in the lobby one night. He informed me that his agent had just closed on a deal for the film rights with Universal (disposition and negotiation of subsidiary rights is the author's province, not the producer's). I had admired Tom for being loyal to his longtime, second-tier "boutique" agent when this, his first success, came along, but when he told me the specifics of the deal, I went ballistic on him. His agent had tied the amounts of advances he would receive to the length of the Broadway run. In other words, if the Broadway production was performing marginally, Universal might be more motivated to close it if an escalator payment was coming due.

Topor had been determined that we assign the rights to a producer with deep pockets who could keep the show running and promote it more when the box office lagged, then he signed a deal which gave that producer motivation not to do that. He was too savvy to have agreed to this, but he did.

And, sure, enough, that exact scenario is what came to pass. "Nuts" never did more than hover around its weekly break-even point on Broadway, partly due to a scathing pan by Frank Rich in the *Times*, and, as it was approaching its 100th performance on Broadway, Universal posted a closing notice to shut it down after 96.

To add to the irony (but typical of Hollywood), Universal never ending up making a film of "Nuts." Warner Brothers did. Starring Barbra Streisand and Richard Dreyfuss. It was released seven years later, and Topor was one of three screenwriters credited with the adaptation.

When compared to Hollywood, Broadway often looks sane.

That June, as "Nuts" played its final weeks and I was consumed with pre-production for my Minnesota adventure, the WPA opened its season finale, a small, engaging coming-of-age play by David Rimmer about four high schoolers in the 1960s, entitled "Album."

Rich himself reviewed the WPA production for the *Times* (rare for the most influential paper's first-string critic), perhaps because it was staged by film director Joan Micklin Silver and one of its quartet of actors was Keith Gordon, a hot young actor who at the time was receiving raves for his pivotal role in the Brian De Palma film "Home Movies." Whatever Rich's motivation for coming, he wrote a valentine to the play, as well as to Gordon; his one regret was that the play's running time was only 90 minutes...not that he felt it needed more fleshing out, but because he was enjoying the characters' company so much.

There isn't much to say about its transfer because everything was done right and there was no craziness. Gene Persson, who had co-produced the original off-Broadway production of "You're a Good Man, Charlie Brown" in 1967 signed on as the lead producer. The production was so modest that it fit comfortably into the 199-seat Cherry Lane Theatre in the Village, where it ran for 257 performances.

The entire cast consisted of two men and two women, who were rightfully praised as an ensemble, not just by Rich, but by all the critics. Gordon received almost all of the individual accolades. The other young male (and equal) presence on stage was hardly mentioned. His name was Kevin Bacon.

It looked as if the WPA's 1980-81 season would be our first without a commercial transfer. By spring, there was only one more production to mount, and, with very little money left in the season's budget (as usual), Kyle found a three-character comedy about New York singles discussing relationships and commitment while bicycling together in Central Park. Called "Key Exchange," it was sufficiently well-crafted by first-time playwright Kevin Wade that Kyle and I expressed the hope to each other that we could close out the season on a quiet, respectable note without too much dismissive criticism.

Rich had other ideas, though. This time the allure that brought him to the WPA was probably the actress Brooke Adams, who had made a proverbial splash in the films "Days of Heaven" and "Invasion of the Body Snatchers." In his *Times* review, he swooned over both her and the play. And the commercial transfer machinery went into motion once again.

It was clearly an off-Broadway play, and several off-Broadway producers jumped into the ring to produce it together. In one corner, there were Mitchell Maxwell and Alan Schuster, who were principals in the company that owned the Orpheum, which is where "Key Exchange" would move. In the other corner, there was the father-son team of Frank and Mark Gero, who back then were better known as Liza Minnelli's father-in-law and husband, respectively.

And it isn't a coincidence that I use the boxing analogy. Let's just say it wasn't the most harmonious of partnerships. Kyle and I had to do a tag-team in dealing with the principals on this one, even after its Orpheum opening.

Part of the contract we had negotiated called for them to turn the theatre over to us one night for a benefit performance, which meant all proceeds from that performance would go to the WPA. But one (or more) of the producers devised a scheme to get around having to sacrifice a night of ticket sales. They told us they would abide by the contract, but since the contract didn't specify a start time for the performance, they had decided to make it 10 p.m., following the regular performance. To accomplish this, they claimed they'd find a way to get a dispensation from Actors' Equity to have nine shows that week instead of the usual eight.

Obviously, the type of people who shell out extra money to attend a benefit performance, especially on a weeknight, aren't going to come to an event that begins at 10 p.m., so Kyle and I each tried to drive a wedge into the already splintered team of producers in order to get sanity to prevail. Ultimately we did, with an assist from Jeremy Nussbaum, who provided us with practical as well as legal advice. Even so, on Jeremy's orders, Kyle and I didn't arrive at the Orpheum on the night of the benefit until the house lights had gone down, just so a last-minute surprise couldn't be sprung on us.

Unbelievable, the games that get played.

Success Indeed Has Many Fathers

Howard Ashman had turned 10 years-old the year that Roger Corman's low-budget, "Grade B" horror/comedy film "The Little Shop of Horrors" opened in theatres. Sometime in his early teen years he began to think of it as the possible basis for a musical. He never forgot it and, as the film went on to achieve cult status as one of those cinematic efforts that fans laugh *at*, not with, Howard began to take adapting it into a stage musical more seriously.

And so it was that it became his next project following the disappointment of "God Bless You, Mr. Rosewater," leading to a production of it at the WPA in May of 1982.

Many hit musicals announce themselves as such well before opening night. There's an aura surrounding them, usually stemming from word-of-mouth within the industry based on rehearsal or early preview buzz. "Little Shop of Horrors" was one of these. There was never any doubt.

Since I had long ceased to have daily involvement at the WPA, I first became exposed to it at a preview performance at the WPA. And the offers from commercial producers were already coming in.

Kyle, Jeremy, and I began fielding them and having almost daily discussions. There was never any doubt that Howard would make the final decision, but it was our responsibility to evaluate the plethora of offers and to make sure the WPA got the best deal it could.

Kyle had already hired veteran off-Broadway general manager Albert Poland to serve that function on the impending commercial production; it was our intent that WPA become an indemnified general partner on the commercial producing team. I didn't know

Poland (never did meet him, in fact, same as with Alan Menken) and I was never party to interactions with him, but, given his long-standing relationship with the Shuberts, he was lobbying them in conjunction with Kyle. Apparently, Bernie Jacobs hadn't been a huge fan of the show, although he realized its commercial potential. Kyle, Jeremy, and I decided in conversation that I would focus on cultivating Jujamcyn, which had also expressed interest. It was clear early on that one of those two Broadway theatre chains would be the linchpin of any deal.

There's little argument that theatre owners doubling as producers had become necessary when the costs of opening a show on Broadway had reached the point that many independent producers needed assistance in putting together a show's capitalization. I have always been of two minds about how healthy this is as an industry practice, but in the case of "Little Shop," it wasn't about needing money – plenty of that was being thrown at us from every direction. It was about the most stability for the show, the best associations that could benefit Howard and Alan in their careers, and the best ongoing financial participation the WPA could negotiate. It was this last item that Jeremy, Kyle, and I needed to focus on as sort of an ad hoc executive committee of the corporation's board, whose mission was to protect and advance the WPA's interests.

Some of what was offered us, or asked for, was downright absurd. For instance, an executive from Paramount called Kyle and, in addition to the usual elements of an assignment of rights deal, offered the WPA seven-and-a-half percent of the Gulf+Western building on Columbus Circle. Huh? He had somehow calculated that if they converted the ground level movie theatre in front of the main building into a small legit theatre and gave us exclusive use of it (not that we wanted it), that would equate to seven-and-a-half percent of the whole building. (By coincidence, I was dating his cousin at the time, and she confirmed that he was an idiot.)

Another laughable call came from the agent of the actress Ellen Greene, who played Audrey, the female lead. Apparently, Greene wanted to "copyright" her character. Again, huh? Actors can't copyright characters they play, and, besides, she was playing a dumb blonde, hardly an original character type. Kyle dispensed with this inquiry as diplomatically as he could.

In all, there were about two dozen expressions of interest from commercial entities, and most looked pretty much the same. It quickly came down to the substance of the suitor, which led us back to Shubert and Jujamcyn.

The fact they were vying for a show that was destined to open off-Broadway (the Orpheum in the East Village was the perfect venue for it), yet they both owned multiple larger theatres in the Broadway district, naturally raised suspicion about what their ultimate intent might be. After his horrible experience with "God Bless You, Mr. Rosewater" getting lost in a theatre that was too big for it, Howard didn't want to take any chance of that happening with "Little Shop" at any point in the future, and the rest of us agreed with that wholeheartedly. This led to our one non-negotiable point in assigning the rights; we dubbed it the "unilateral move clause," which essentially meant that the theatre owner couldn't on its own decide to move the show to Broadway. Such a move could only be made with the approval of Howard and the WPA.

For "Little Shop" to really work, the audience, at the end, has to *believe* the plant is devouring the world, and Howard's masterstroke (expertly executed by Hawk Gianfrancesco) of having vines fall out of drop-boxes all over the audience during the final number can only be accomplished in a small space. Put the fully-grown plant and only a modicum of falling vines in a cavernous theatre and the effect is laughably ridiculous, as has been proven by the several productions that have tried this throughout the decades. Even at the Orpheum, a narrow but deep theatre, it didn't have quite the impact it did at the 100-seat WPA.

I met with Dick Wolff, the president of Jujamcyn at the time, and when the subject of our one non-negotiable demand came up, he resisted. He promised he wouldn't unilaterally move the show uptown to one of his theatres, but he didn't want to put it in writing. "If we're trusting you, we want you to trust us about not moving it to Broad-WAAAY," was his refrain. (Dick would always put the emphasis on the second syllable of the word). But what he said made no sense because how was *he* trusting us?

There were conversations between us that followed, and Howard even met with him on his own, later telling Kyle that he'd never met anyone so paranoid about being undermined by his rival. But it wasn't the Shuberts that were undermining him; it was Dick himself.

WPA's percentage of net profits kept rising during the talks, finally reaching an unprecedented level for a non-profit theatre assigning commercial rights. The Shuberts' final offer reached 35% of net. Wanting to one-up Bernie Jacobs – but misreading the dynamic of the situation – Dick offered 40%. Of course, this was in addition to the customary percentage of weekly gross the WPA received as the originating producer.

The Shuberts had no problem with the clause we insisted on. They also brought in the reigning king of musical producers, Cameron Mackintosh, and recording titan David Geffen to create a powerhouse team above the title, so the decision became academic in the end.

Howard would now be in the A-list company he sought. Perplexingly, though, his talent never came to be appreciated to the degree it deserved to be by the Broadway community. He and Marvin Hamlisch struggled to get "Smile" to Broadway after the Shuberts dropped out following a workshop production. He never became the "go to" name when a show needed a bookwriter, or if it needed fixing. Was it because he had developed a reputation as someone who could be difficult to work with, as several actors have said? He surely wasn't the first, and his creative gift for musical theatre was pretty much unparalleled at the time. Plus, he had already written and directed a smash hit.

Thing is, Howard always viewed himself as a guy knocking on the door of the inner circle, waiting for it open, knowing it should but believing it probably wouldn't. This is reflected in a comment he once gave to an interviewer:

"'Little Shop,'" he said, "would never have been produced had I not had my own theatre. In order to reach the public, it had to get past the New York theatre establishment." (I disagree with this; getting it done would have been harder, but somewhere along the line some producer or non-profit theatre would have seen its merit and commercial potential.)

Regardless, I've always maintained there are two people from whom I learned the most about musical-making. One, unsurprisingly, was Hal Prince. The other was Howard. And I elevate him to that pedestal despite what were, ultimately, my several personal misgivings about him.

Ironically, in Hollywood (or, more precisely, Burbank), he did finally find the full appreciation of his talent that had eluded him in New York. And that a company like Disney would be the one to embrace him and give him the large degree of creative control they did is more than a little startling given the legendary egos of Jeffrey Katzenberg and Michael Eisner. But they were smart enough to realize what Broadway power brokers hadn't: that Howard was more than just a songwriter they happened to hire; he was a generational talent with an auteur's vision, which is exactly what they needed to resurrect the studio's tattered reputation in animation.

From all accounts, he became "key man" in the making of both "The Little Mermaid" and "Beauty and the Beast." Having known Howard as well as I did, I can state with certainty that he would have hated every change that was made when, following his death from AIDS in 1991, "Beauty" was adapted for Broadway. What he would have most objected to were the added songs that "stepped on" other, better songs from the film and altered the structure in a way that diluted the story's impact. He also would have hated that the show's *raison d'etre* was arguably to further capitalize on the name value of the franchise without enhancing it in any way. Had he been alive, Howard might have gone along with adapting it for Broadway, but it would have been carried out with far greater integrity and talent.

None of this, of course, would even have happened had it not been for "Little Shop" finally providing Howard with the success he had worked so hard to achieve through so many disappointments. But hit shows have a way of creating happy outcomes for everyone even tangentially associated with them.

The outcome for the WPA was that it had no financial woes for many years until, finally, the theme of our board meetings became how to survive when the "Little Shop" percentages and profits began to fall off.

As for me, the outcome was that Jujamcyn offered me a newly created position as its Director of Creative Development. It seems Dick Wolff had been impressed with me in our one meeting and several phone conversations and, with my dear and loyal friend Howard Rogut advocating for me on the inside, I received an offer. Thanks to "Little Shop" – which I had very little to do with, and nothing creatively – I was now going, in a significant way, to where I had always wanted to be.

Broadway.

The Jujamcyn Years

Welcome to Broad-WAAAY

At the time I came aboard, Jujamcyn was owned by a man named James Binger, a former president and chairman of Honeywell, Inc., and his wife, Virginia, the daughter of William L. McKnight, the transformational 20-year president and, subsequently, 17-year chairman of the 3M Corporation during its biggest growth years. McKnight had bought the St. James Theatre in 1956 and the Martin Beck (now the Al Hirschfeld) Theatre a decade later. He named the company for the Bingers' three children, Judith, James, and Cynthia. Following McKnight's death in 1978, Binger took over control of the company and three years later set about buying three more Broadway theatres: the Eugene O'Neill, the ANTA (which would be renamed the Virginia, after his wife, and is now the August Wilson), and what would become the Ritz (which is now the Walter Kerr).

At the time, Binger had five homes in various corners of the world, including his principal one in Minneapolis and a large apartment in New York at the Sherry-Netherland Hotel at 59th Street and Fifth Avenue. Authors of shows that were lobbying Jujamcyn for a booking would often be invited to audition their material for us at this apartment with a postcard view of Central Park. Beautiful as the view was, though, a guest's sensibilities could be jolted by a few of the, well, quirks in Binger's aesthetic choices in interior design.

When you entered his apartment, the first thing you saw in his front hallway was a life-size sculpture of a naked, bleached blonde woman wearing a sailor cap, leaning over and mooning you. (No, I'm not kidding.)

The apartment also featured a Steinway grand piano that for some inexplicable reason had been painted British racing green. When Kander and Ebb auditioned the score for their Chita Rivera-Liza Minelli musical "The Rink" there, Kander appeared shell-shocked when he first saw it, and grumbled to me about it as he and I were tasked with turning the piano around (without scraping the floor, please) so he could face the room while playing.

Rumor had it that Bernie Jacobs had recommended to Binger that he hire Dick Wolff to be Jujamcyn's president. It's hard to believe, though, that a businessman of Binger's stature would go with the recommendation of his chief competitor. (But, if true, it would explain a lot, as you will see.)

Binger left the day-to-day operation of the company and its theatres to Dick and his (supercilious) controller, Aldo Scrofani, and would only fly in from his home in Minneapolis (he had four others, including his pad at the Sherry) every month or so to be brought up to date, to see new shows that had opened, and perhaps to accompany Dick to a significant lunch meeting.

The month before I began my Jujamcyn tenure, Dick and Binger had had such a meeting with Alan Jay Lerner about booking Lerner and Charles Strouse's new musical, "Dance a Little Closer," which Lerner himself would direct, into the St. James. Upon my arrival at Jujamcyn, I heard from several people in the office that, at the lunch, Dick and Binger had not only agreed to book the show into their flagship theatre, but to provide a million dollars toward the capitalization. A handshake deal had supposedly been made.

While I was still in the process of settling into my new position, Dick called me into his office and asked me to read Lerner's script and give him my assessment. I wanted to read it in one sitting in a place where I wouldn't be interrupted.

My first office at Jujamcyn was just off the mezzanine in the Ritz Theatre, where renovations were nearing completion. I recall sitting in a mezzanine seat in the empty theatre one afternoon that

September reading the script and not believing my eyes. Both book and lyrics were abysmal. No constructive criticism could help salvage them.

A sadness overcame me as I thought of all the inspired work that Lerner had given the American musical theatre and the respect I personally had for his talent. And then my thoughts turned inward. I began questioning what right did *I* have to trash a work of his and possibly impede it from reaching Broadway? I had never hesitated to be brutal in my assessments when it was called for, but somehow this was different. This required a true soul-searching, which I sat in the Ritz mezzanine and did.

I finally accepted what I had to do, knowing full well the implications of my sharing my strong negative opinion with Dick. I walked the four blocks to 44th Street, went into Dick's office, and opened the window.

"I'm afraid you might as well throw the million dollars out there," I said.

I tried to make it not seem as big a deal as it was, noting that Binger could afford the loss and that at least Dick had a booking for the spring. But I got the sense that he had received the same response from the one or two others he had asked to review the project and knew that his and Binger's conversation with Lerner had been premature and had progressed farther than it should have. He was agitated but not livid, which I soon learned he would often become. He did, however, begin saying that he and Binger hadn't made a firm commitment, but had just told Lerner they would *consider* making a million-dollar investment.

A few weeks passed and no further discussion of "Dance a Little Closer" occurred. Then one day I was in the outer office and my eye caught a letter written on Lerner's personal stationery lying on top of a filing cabinet. I started reading and it soon became obvious that Dick had indeed told Lerner that he and Binger had never made a commitment and that Jujamcyn wouldn't be participating in his show. Lerner ended his brief note with a line that I've never forgotten:

"I may have only one eye, but I have two ears, and I know what I heard," Lerner wrote.

Deep down, I did too.

I took little satisfaction when "Close a Little Faster," as it had been dubbed on the street, did just that. After its opening (and closing) night performance in a Nederlander theatre.

Abdications

When I first entered the business right out of college, I didn't understand why any producer would option a property to produce commercially and then not see it through to fruition unless the money simply couldn't be raised to put it on. I soon learned there are any number of reasons for abandonment, some even before an option agreement can be drawn up and others during a play's development, as you will see in this and coming chapters, and it occurs much more often than not.

There were two scripts I had been haunted by for a few years before I joined Jujamcyn. The first of these was a play by a gentle, talented lady named Ruth Wolff (no relation to Dick) and was called "The Abdication." It can best be described as historical fiction written on a grand theatrical scale that served to put contemporary feminist issues into stark relief through the religious and romantic challenges of its seventeenth century protagonist, Queen Christina of Sweden.

Surprisingly, it had been Sleaze who had brought the play to my attention years prior when Ruth had been represented by Audrey Wood, whom I have already referenced as one of the two great women of theatre that I feel privileged to have had the opportunity just to meet, let alone, in Ms. Wood's case, to have substantive dealings with. One of the walls of her ICM office featured framed copies of the awards won by her most famous client, Tennessee Williams, who had left her for another agent, an act that it was clear had hurt her immensely.

My two most vivid memories of Ms. Wood all happened during discussions with her about "The Abdication" when I had first optioned it while working with Sleaze and Dilettante, prior to Ms. Wood's incapacitation. As anyone who dealt with Ms. Wood can attest, my experiences with her on phone conversations were not unique. I would start to end a conversation with the usual niceties…and she would have already hung up. And what I'll most remember is in what turned out to be our last phone conversation, during which we had conversed about the future of Broadway, her closing words to me, spoken with genuine warmth before abruptly hanging up, were "God bless you."

As for "The Abdication," the stumbling block for commercial producers was that, following its British premiere in 1971 by the Bristol Old Vic Company, the film rights had immediately been gobbled up, with Wolff hired to write the screenplay. Anthony Harvey, coming off his successful film adaptation of "The Lion in Winter" was hired to direct, and Liv Ullman and Peter Finch were cast in the two lead roles. The end product, though, released in 1974, was almost unwatchable and failed miserably. My own feeling is that what makes the play so special is its innate theatricality, which is all but impossible to replicate, or compensate for, in the film medium. Many successful plays should just be left alone and not made into films for this very reason. "A Chorus Line" serves as the poster child of my generation as an example of why this is so.

I wasn't overly fazed by this drawback and neither were the three new producing partners I found to join us. Peter Neufeld was brought on as general manager. Andre Ernotte had a strong vision for the production and was hired to direct. I sent the script to Meryl Streep, who was perfect for Christina; she passed due to other commitments but did so in a lovely note to me that said she had been familiar with the play, had loved it, and thanked me for sending it. Then, one of our producing partners or Neufeld (I can't recall which) got it to Vanessa Redgrave, who was gung-ho to do it. Neufeld took it upon himself to negotiate the parameters of a viable deal with her agent, subject to our final approval.

It was now time to meet with Dick to discuss the timeline for fundraising; with each party in for $250,000, we figured it shouldn't be too hard given a major star's commitment. But as soon as the meeting in Dick's office began, he threw up a roadblock, saying that he had been thinking and was concerned by what a politically controversial figure Redgrave was at the time and had become worried that someone might set off a bomb in the theatre. (I wanted to point out that recently he had been pretty good at doing that himself, but I refrained.) He nervously explained that he was responsible for the safe-keeping of Binger's theatres and that he simply couldn't run the risk of having such a volatile star appearing in one of them…and thus Jujamcyn would be pulling out.

We all sat there dumbfounded. The three other partners felt betrayed and their frostiness was evident as they exited Dick's office. I was still in shock, but, at that early point in my tenure at Jujamcyn, I viewed Dick's bizarre withdrawal as a one-off.

With the play's New York future very uncertain, Redgrave proposed to Ruth Wolff that they prep the play for a West End production instead, and Ruth flew over to London to work with her. Redgrave herself acquired the British stage rights, so she was now calling the shots.

A short while later, I got a call from Ruth in London saying that Redgrave wanted numerous changes to make the play more overtly political and that she didn't set out, nor at this point desired, to write polemic. As an actress working under a director's guidance, Redgrave would probably have been excellent, but once she controlled the property, she wanted it to be a vehicle for her to make strong socio-political statements. After Ruth pulled out and flew home, though, the project evaporated.

A few years later, one of my final acts as an employee of Jujamcyn was to fly to Cincinnati to see another of Ruth's plays, this one entitled "Empress of China." It, too, was fascinating historical fiction and had been given a breathtaking staging by Robert Kalfin.

Like "The Abdication," it deserved to make it to Broadway but never did. Simply put, a loss.

The other script that had haunted me from my pre-Jujamcyn days was a three-character comedy that the agent Howard Rosenstone had sent me, perhaps not aware that I was no longer involved with the WPA on a day-to-day basis. It was by a Yale School of Drama graduate named David Epstein and was about a couple dealing with marital commitment and possible infertility.

Since I couldn't get it out of my mind, I made it one of the first properties I put into development in my new position on West 44th Street. I knew it needed more work, but I had trouble figuring out why it didn't add up to a wholly satisfying play. Epstein agreed with me that we had to get a director on board for him to work with, so I started sending it around to likely suspects. I also sent a copy to my friend John Rubinstein, who was one of the most intelligent actors I had ever known and was also perfect for the one male role. He responded with enthusiasm and a desire to do it.

So did one of the first directors on our list, Melvin Bernhardt, whose prior Broadway credits included Beth Henley's "Crimes of the Heart" and Hugh Leonard's "Da," both of which had won him Tonys for Best Director to the latter of which had won him a Tony for Best Director in 1978. I arranged for him to meet Epstein and each reported back that they would work wonderfully together. Bernhardt wanted to put together a reading of the play at his Upper West Side apartment, for which he was able to recruit Karen Allen and Swoozie Kurtz for the two female roles, with Rubinstein rounding out the cast.

The three were perfect and the cold reading went smoothly, especially the short first act in which the play is at its funniest. It was clear that, while the second and third acts held one's interest, they were a letdown after the first. But the promise of the project was never higher. I went about finding a place for "Bedrock" to have a tryout production (or what Dick Wolff always referred to as "a cheap look-see") while Epstein and Bernhardt went to work refining the script.

Or so I thought. Bernhardt resisted producorial involvement in his creative process, which frustrated me as a creative producer but which I didn't fight. At least he didn't want me to leave the state, as Gower Champion once demanded of David Merrick, or, worse, the country, as Bob Fosse made the "Pippin" writers do when taping a production of that show in Canada. In the case of "Bedrock," I wasn't too worried because the two collaborators got along so well.

I had developed a friendship with Craig Anderson, whom the New York press had made the "golden boy" of off-Broadway when he was Producing Director of the Hudson Guild Theater in the late '70s. In a sense, I had envied Craig for the endless publicity he got while I had felt anonymous at the WPA despite having fathered it, but then I had never put myself front and center as he had. When we met, we hit it off immediately and were anxious to work on a project together. He read and liked "Bedrock" and came aboard as a co-producer. And, indeed, working with Craig turned out to be a joy.

We found another fan of the play in Ed Sherin, who at the time was Artistic Director of the Hartman Theatre in Stamford, Connecticut. He offered us a slot in his upcoming season, which we grabbed. Rubinstein indicated he was definitely in, but, as much as we wanted the two actresses from the reading in Bernhardt's apartment, both Allen and Kurtz were otherwise committed for our production dates in January, 1984.

Casting the role Allen had played was fairly easy; Anne Twomey, late of "Nuts," was both available and interested, and she was an ideal fit for the role.

An intriguing prospect for the other female role presented itself. I received a call from David Guc, an agent whom I had known and liked, telling me his client Kathleen Turner would be interested, even though it was a supporting role. What was odd was that this happened after the film "Body Heat" had made her a star.

Guc explained that she wanted to work in theatre but was looking to start in a supporting role in a low-pressure situation outside New York. Fair enough. And Guc was in a position to know; he and Turner had lived together in the late '70s. I forget why, but I had happened to have a phone conversation with him on the day she was moving out a few years prior, and he was pretty bummed. I commiserated with him and said it must be doubly painful to lose someone who was an important client as well as a lover.

He responded that, no, he was keeping her as a client. "I figure if I can't have a hundred percent of her, I might as well keep ten," he quipped.

For "Bedrock," he offered to have her read for us in his office. It was more than slightly awkward, and none of us was overwhelmed, Bernhardt least of all. Craig and I had our own reason for deciding to pass on her: it would have created an imbalance in the production, especially with the biggest name of the three playing the smallest role.

And so we held one afternoon of auditions and ended up hiring a superb actress named Jean DeBaer. Yet what I remember most was a heartbreaking episode. John Rubinstein's actress wife at the time had asked to audition. None of us knew that their relationship might be in trouble. But in the middle of her reading, she broke down and, through tears, said "Please, hire me. I need to keep my marriage together."

Sometimes real life intrudes and knocks you broadside.

Rehearsals began and, true to form, Bernhardt kept them closed to producers. He and Epstein regularly reported, though, that all was going great. But when Craig and I were finally allowed in to see a run-through, we were shocked. Nothing had changed. No script revisions had been made. Bernhardt and Epstein seemed unconcerned, but both expressed annoyance with the actors. Bernhardt referred to them as "children." For their part, the three actors were testy with him. And we were about to leave for final rehearsals on the stage in Stamford.

"Suddenly it all came back to me," Craig said when we were alone. Bernhardt had directed "Da" for him at Hudson Guild, and despite that production's eventual Broadway success, Craig recalled a similar problem early on. He had just blocked it out of his consciousness until now. He had concluded that Bernhardt essentially "freezes" his interpretation and staging before rehearsals start and that, once they do, he becomes inflexible to changes.

Apparently he had also convinced Epstein that the script was perfect as is, that no revisions were needed. According to Rubinstein, Bernhardt wouldn't even answer the actors' questions and would simply tell them to do what he told them. Craig and I knew that, working with three of the most intelligent actors in New York theatre, this was NOT a viable approach.

In Stamford, Craig and I decided to start by dealing with each camp separately. The first night we had dinner with Mel and David, who railed on about how impossible these actors were, always asking questions and arguing over every little thing. We hoped our suggestions about trying to meet them halfway and be more responsive would be listened to and attempted, late in the game as it was. But by that point, the resentments were running deep and each of the two camps had firmly staked its ground.

The next night, we took the three actors to dinner. Before we ordered, Craig explained that he had worked with their director before and could perhaps be helpful here. Assuming an erudite tone, he said "Now, the way to deal with Melvin…"

Rubinstein interrupted him before he could finish.

"…is to buy a gun and use it."

Without missing a beat, Craig turned and called, "Waiter!" He knew further words would be futile.

For all of this, what ended up on stage at the Hartman was not without a lot of merit. Despite all the behind-the-scenes dissension and division, what the audience saw was thoroughly professional and often engaging. It also provided a surprise that I had no idea was coming despite my familiarity with the script. I was totally unprepared for, but elated by, the gales of laughter that cascaded through Rubinstein's third act speech graphically describing the indignities and discomfort he experienced having a male fertility examination earlier that day.

I say it was in the third act, but for most of the run it was in the second. After opening night, we combined acts one and two into one act with two scenes. The first act we opened with was simply too short to stand on its own. We all agreed on that, but what I most remember was David Epstein's agent, Howard Rosenstone, browbeating him in the theatre lobby on opening night about it. "You simply can't do that to an audience," Rosenstone scolded. Fair enough, until I saw David Mamet's "Glengarry Glen Ross" on Broadway a few months later with a first act that was equally brief. Rosenstone was also Mamet's agent and I wondered if he had rebuked *that* client of his the same way he had Epstein. Somehow I doubt it.

Had more work been done on "Bedrock" so it paid off dramatically in the end, it could have been a hit. As it was, it got respectful but largely mixed-to-negative notices that raised no one's blood pressure. Alvin Klein perhaps summed it up best in his *Times* review, concluding, "The play promises more than it delivers, but at least it delivers something of sustenance for a time." I found it hard to argue with that.

Tune, Twiggy, & Ice

Once settled in my role as Director of Creative Development, I went about connecting with all the theatre lit agents in town to tell them what I was up to. I knew the majority of them from my prior travels, but even if I didn't, they took my calls promptly.

Well, almost. I called one of the veteran battleaxes at a major agency (an agent I knew only from humorously mocking industry impersonations of her voice) and introduced myself to the young Cerberus who answered her phone.

"Head of Creative at Ju—what?," he asked.

"Jujamcyn," I replied pleasantly. "The theatre owner."

"Oh, just a second," he said, putting me on hold.

About thirty seconds later he came back on the line. "Could you tell me what theatre you own?," he asked, obviously at his boss' behest.

"Well," I said, "the St. James, Eugene O'Neill, Martin Beck, Virginia, and Ritz."

There was a pause. "Just a second," he said for the second time, placing me on hold again.

Almost immediately, Her Nibs picked up the phone, bright and obsequious as could be. "Oh, helllllloooo, Mr. Wells."

What this little episode told me was that either this pseudo-*grande dame* had downed one too many vodka stingers at lunch that day or the "major player" company I had just begun working for – in my dream job, a Broadway executive position that people all over the theatre landscape would kill to have – had a major PR problem. There were only three Broadway theatre chains; how could a top agent *not know the name of one of them*? I pushed it out of my mind quickly enough, unaware that it was a harbinger of the revelations about Jujamcyn that were to hit me broadside within the next year.

Regardless, I took her to lunch one day soon after that, as I had long previously learned that the only way to get an agent's attention is to meet with them somewhere other than their offices where there are constant interruptions and distractions. During this introductory agent tour of mine though, there was one – Luis Sanjurjo of ICM – who refused to let me take him to lunch and instead insisted that I come to him.

Sanjurjo, in his early forties, was with ICM, and had inherited many of Audrey Wood's well-known clients the prior year upon that iconic agent's incapacitation following the severe stroke that eventually led to her death. (Sanjurjo himself, sadly, would die of cancer in 1987.) To say his style was unlike hers would be grossly understating the reality.

I arrived for our meeting and served my mandatory sentence in the ICM waiting area before Luis' assistant came to fetch me. When I arrived at Luis' door, he was sitting prissily behind his desk. He didn't get up to greet me, so I walked over to shake his hand, and then sat down. I tried to be conversational, but I sensed he wasn't interested in anything I had to say. Finally, there came a point when I was silent and he was forced to say *something*.

"I have no idea what it is that you people are looking for," he said coolly. "We brought you our best project, our Tommy Tune and Twiggy musical, and you had no interest in it, so I don't know *what* you might like."

Obviously, this had happened before I came aboard the Good Ship Jujamcyn. I knew nothing about what had transpired, and, truth be known, really didn't care since Jujamcyn had already passed. Also, while I had heard about the show he was referencing, I didn't know very much about this "new" Gershwin musical that would eventually become "My One and Only."

But one thing was clear: The meeting I was in had tanked, and nothing I could say would change the attitude Luis was projecting. So I bit my tongue, refrained from calling him an arrogant, short-sighted twit, and tap-danced my way to the abortive end of the meeting. As I left his office, I couldn't help but ponder how Ms. Wood would feel about Luis now handling so many of the clients she treasured.

This turned out to be only my first of many experiences with "My One and Only."

Jump cut forward a few months, and suddenly the show is mostly financed, with Paramount as its chief backer. Dick Wolff gets a call from Tommy Tune's chief agent at ICM, Eric Schepard. It seems that ICM's most powerful agent, Sam Cohn, had taken enough time away from his habit of chewing huge wads of Kleenex to put together the entire producing and theatre package for the show to open at the Palace, which is owned by the Nederlander Organization. Schepard's problem is that *his* client, Tune, wants the St. James.

Now you're probably wondering, since all the agents involved are at ICM, why don't they just get together and sort this out? Well, it doesn't quite work that way in the political world of Broadway. You see, nobody at ICM really wants to upset Sam, because a) it might come back to haunt them as they need his help on other projects they're shepherding, and b) his Kleenex consumption might go up. And who knows what other show Sam might be leveraging as part of the deal to get the Nederlanders in the loop on "My One and Only"? So all this is taking place without the knowledge of the artist who's the driving force (Tune) and will be presented to him as a *fait accompli*. Thus, in order to protect his own client's interests, Schepard has to seek an outside ally to stab his fellow agent in the back for him.

And Dick, for his part, is now interested in the show because it is mostly financed, with Paramount Theatre Productions as lead producers, and could be an attractive booking for his flagship theatre.

I get an urgent call to come to Dick's office.

"Steve, I need you to get Tommy Tune's home number for me," he states with impatience.

Notice he *doesn't* say, "Do you think you might be able to get Tommy Tune's number for me?" He just assumes I can. Heads of companies tend to think that way. Years later, when I was working in network television development for The Hearst Corporation, a directive came down to me from one of their senior board members to "create a breakout character."

Oh, sure thing, Ben. No prob. I'll stop goofing off and have one for you by morning.

But Dick's directive was somewhat easier to fulfill; fortunately, I had an idea as to how I could get Tune's number and within an hour I was able to give it to him. He called Tune immediately.

"Tommy, we can't wait for you to come back to Broad-WAAAY," Dick began. "But I thought you'd want to know that Sam Cohn is about to close a deal with the Nederlanders to put your show into the Palace."

Tune confirmed he had told *his* agent he wanted the St. James.

"Then you better call Sam right away and put a stop to it. We'd *love* to have you at the James," Dick assured him.

An hour passed. All other work stopped as we sat around Dick's office waiting to see how this intrigue played itself out. Then Dick got the inevitable call from Sam Cohn.

"You upset Jimmy's and my apple cart," Sam tells him disgustedly.

"I have my own apple cart to worry about, Sam," Dick shoots back. Then they hurl insults back and forth at each other for a few minutes, after which Dick, feeling victorious, laughs and hangs up.

Shortly afterward, a deal is made to open the show at the St. James in the spring, with Jujamcyn investing $100,000 as "end money."

But it turns out that all was not going swimmingly in Gershwin-land. By the time the show opened its tryout in Boston in February, 1983, its esoteric Harvard "wunderkind" director Peter Sellars had been fired (note: always be wary of Harvard or Yale wunderkinds), the veteran Peter Stone was being brought in to overhaul the book, Mike Nichols was shadow-directing, and the show on stage at the Colonial Theatre was such a mess that Tune felt compelled to give an apologetic curtain speech from the stage at every performance.

As word of this chaos reached New York (which happened before the curtain on the first performance came down in Boston), the doomsayers were out in force. And this served to make Dick even more of a nervous wreck than he usually was anyway. At one point I made the mistake of trying to put it all in perspective for him ("You only have a small investment in it, and you have no control over its future, so why worry so much?"). All this did was only get him more red-faced and agitated.

But Dick wasn't the only one panicking. The Paramount executives were as well. They were threatening to pull the plug following the Boston run.

And so, one morning I got a call from Dick's assistant, Annette, telling me to be at the Minskoff Studios that afternoon for a command run-through of the new first act that Stone and Nichols had put together in an all-out salvage effort. I was informed that it would be on the basis of this run-through that Paramount would decide whether to continue with the project or pull out.

I arrived at the rehearsal studio at the appointed time and the "suits" were all lined up in a single row against the western wall, each wearing a "show me" expression on his face. The tension they created in the room was palpable. No one was smiling. Not even close. Except for one person, and that was Maury Yeston, whose prior year's Broadway musical, "Nine," had been directed by Tune, and who was there due to that relationship and perhaps because he's an incessantly upbeat personality.

"Hi, Wells. I saw some of what Stone and Nichols have done and it's brilliant you're going to love it I gave Nichols a few suggestions for the music and he said Yeston you're a genius but then he's probably heard that from Tune who loves me and Stone what can you say he's Stone…"

Thanks, Maury.

Of course, my opinion, Dick's opinion, others from Jujamcyn's opinion, Yeston's opinion all mean nothing. In fact, I'm not even sure why we're all here. Dick only adds to the tension in the room, and as supportive as the rest of us try to appear, we can't counteract the aura created by the "suits."

Then Mike Nichols addresses all of us and does one of the most astonishing things I've ever seen a director do.

"I have only two things to say before we begin," he started. "First, some of the new material you'll be seeing was just put in this morning, so be aware of that. And second, to the cast: Just relax, everything's on the line."

Incredibly, once he said that, once he acknowledged the truth of the situation, the unbearable tension in the room lifted. And the actors could stop dwelling on the stakes and focus on performing the material. (I later learned this was a common tactic of his.) As the saying goes, I guess he didn't get where he got by being dumb.

And the run-through came off smoothly, without a major glitch.

The "suits" didn't bail and the show would go on.

Still, as the May 1st opening night approached, Dick created his own special brand of tension. To be around him you'd think Jujamcyn's last dime was riding on whether "My One and Only" was a hit. Then again, it was the company's final chance to have a hit open in one of their theatres that season. This isn't to say they hadn't made money in theatre rentals – especially given the way Dick and

Aldo padded the costs that were charged weekly to the productions that occupied its real estate. But when your biggest money-making tenant of the season to that point was also one of the legendary fiascos of all time – "Moose Murders" – you knew you were amassing a resume that didn't look good to your boss.

As it turned out, "My One and Only" did become a modest hit and, more importantly for Dick and Jujamcyn, a long-term tenant at the St. James.

The opening night party was a lavish affair held at the old Tavern on the Green in Central Park. The reason I personally find it memorable is because of something that happened to me while standing in line at the buffet table. Right in front of me was none other than Luis Sanjurjo. He noticed me and his face lit up with delight. He measured his words carefully, punctuating each one with a poke at my chest.

"Well…done…YOU!"

It was clear that in *his* mind our meeting in his office seven months earlier had prompted me to rush back to Jujamcyn and talk some sense into them to get them interested in the show. Of course, that wasn't what happened at all, and in truth I had virtually nothing to do with how Jujamcyn ended up being involved with the show.

My attorney, Jeremy Nussbaum, was standing with me in line. Knowing what had really happened, he whispered in my ear to let Luis keep believing what he wants.

But my defining memory of the "My One and Only" chapter at Jujamcyn – other than occasional reports that would reach us upstairs that Twiggy had fallen off her moon (a free-hanging set piece) yet again – had to do with a mechanical failure in the theatre the following month

It was one of the hottest early Junes on record, and the air-conditioning system at the St. James conked out. Done. Down for the count. Total replacement necessary.

This caused many a hurried and excited meeting in Dick's office between him and Aldo. It seems that part of their employment contracts included annual profit-sharing, determined on a fiscal year ending every June 30. Apparently, for accounting reasons, any maintenance that was done within a given fiscal year had to be charged *to* that fiscal year, thus reducing the profits and their profit-sharing.

Now, a whole new air-conditioning system for a 1,600-seat Broadway theatre was what might be called a big-ticket item. But there was no time for delay; the situation had to be addressed immediately since they finally had a hit playing in one of their houses, and audiences (silly people) expect not to have to perspire for two-and-a-half hours.

Dick and Aldo weren't about to install a new system before July 1, so they put their brains together and came up with a creative short-term solution. (Trust me, I'm not making this up; there are people who can verify it.)

Every morning for the remainder of the month, an ice truck would pull up on West 44th Street outside the St. James and huge blocks of ice would be hauled inside the theatre and positioned so that fans could (theoretically) blow cooling air out into the house.

To say this didn't solve the problem would be an understatement. Audience members would fan themselves with their Playbills, then complain to the house manager, who'd be left to deal with their anger. The cast was up in arms and had no idea which of the many things they were being told they should believe.

For his part, Dick took to hiding, staying at home more days than not. During one seriously hot stretch, Tommy Tune called him at home begging for air, and was intercepted by Dick's obliging wife, Fran, telling him how much they loved him. The wrangling and the excuses went on and on, obviously without anyone letting on as to the real reason only half-baked explanations were forthcoming.

But, of course, this was only a matter of stalling for a couple of weeks and then the new system would be installed and all would be forgiven and forgotten. And Dick and Aldo's profit-sharing wouldn't have suffered.

Indeed, that is what came to pass. But for those several weeks of June, I'd arrive at the office each morning, see the ice truck parked outside the theatre, and think to myself that there were kids all across the country believing that to work in a lofty job on Broadway, as I was, would be to have reached the very pinnacle of professionalism.

Of Pigs, Balloons, & Moguls

A few months prior to my joining Jujamcyn, when Kyle, Jeremy, and I were in the midst of juggling the multitude of commercial transfer offers for "Little Shop of Horrors" to an off-Broadway production, part of what had weighed in the Shuberts' favor was its established partnership with recording mogul David Geffen. Jujamcyn had no such defined music industry affiliation, and that ended up being one of the reasons we didn't assign the rights to them.

So it didn't take a lot of brainpower on my part to realize that if Jujamcyn were to compete for musicals more effectively in the future, it could only help to have a similar relationship in place.

One of the offers WPA had received for "Little Shop" came from legendary record executive Clive Davis, president of Arista Records, who had already been independently dabbling in Broadway producing. He seemed like the perfect person to approach, and I wrote him a brief note suggesting we explore an informal Arista/ Jujamcyn alliance similar to the Geffen/Shubert one that was working so well.

Davis called me immediately upon receiving my note, excited by the prospect and anxious to meet. He invited me to lunch at the Oak Room in the Plaza Hotel, where we met a few days later. He brought with him his A&R chief, Bob Feiden, who himself was a star of sorts in the record world.

After a pleasant discussion, we agreed to proceed to the next step, which was to keep each other apprised of new projects as they came to our individual attention in hopes of finding one or more of mutual interest. We also expressed to each other our desire to try to find a property to develop together with a pop songwriter (an aspiration, as I would later discover, with many inherent obstacles). Walking back to the theatre district from the Plaza, I was excited by all the possibilities that could come from this relationship.

After a few months of having my base of operations be an office in the Ritz, it was decided that I would be re-located to the Virginia Theatre on West 52nd Street, the former ANTA Theatre which had been re-named after Jim Binger's wife (and which is now the August Wilson Theatre). The logic behind my office being there was solid enough – so I could be near the development space that was to be located upstairs – but I wasn't thrilled with being even more isolated, eight blocks north of the main office where all the activity was.

Fairly soon, though, that changed somewhat: A pig moved into the office next to mine. No, not a slob, but a real live oinker. To be precise, a piglet named Michelle, who was in the cast of 83-year-old Eva Le Gallienne's production of "Alice in Wonderland" that was taking up residence at the Virginia. Its producer was an actress named Sabra Jones, who knew how to get what she wanted from Dick by constantly flirting with him and sending balloons to the 44th Street office. He got balloons, I got a pig. And despite this being Ms. Le Gallienne's pig of choice from an audition of six aspiring swine, the production was so large that there was no place to put Michelle when she was "on call" except next door to me.

Anyway, as "Alice" entered its tech week and final rehearsals, one day I was standing at the back of the theatre observing. Suddenly, Howard Rogut came rushing toward me out of nowhere.

"Steve, quick, Clive Davis is on the phone for you!" he whispered with urgency in his voice.

I bolted down the stairs to the lobby and hurried across it to my stall next to Michelle.

When I picked up the phone, Clive got right to the point.

"Have you been to one of Jerry Herman's auditions of 'La Cage Aux Folles' yet?" he asked.

I told him yes, that we had been at Herman's Upper East Side townhouse a few days earlier.

We'll get back to Clive's call in a minute, but first a brief description of backers auditions in general, and the "La Cage" presentation in specific, is called for.

Backers auditions come in all sizes and shapes, some large and professionally sung, others small and often performed by the songwriter(s). The most memorable ones in my experience – of which this was *the* most memorable – are of the latter variety. Sometimes they take place in rehearsal studios, sometimes in a home or apartment. Historically, private rooms at Sardi's have been the most well-known venues, specifically the Belasco Room and, later, the Eugenia Room. The best part of attending auditions at Sardi's was the easy access to their stiff drinks which went a long way toward easing the pain of most auditions.

And that is what it is…pain. At least the vast majority of the time. Sometimes the material is interesting, or shows potential, but rarely does it soar with consummate professionalism and understanding of the commercial musical theatre idiom.

The "La Cage" auditions took place in Jerry Herman's study, on one of the upper floors of his townhouse. There were separate presentations for each of the three Broadway theatre chains, and the only thing that weighed at all in Jujamcyn's favor was that it owned the St. James, which had been home to Herman's "Hello, Dolly!" back in the '60s. ("My One and Only" had not been booked into it yet for the following spring.)

There were less than 25 people squeezed into the room, and I found a perch on a stairway at the back of the room. Dick, of course, fawned all over Herman.

"Jer-rrr-eee, you know how much we'd love to have you back at the James," he gushed. Of course, Jer-rrr-eee knew, as others of his stature always did, that had he written a show that didn't have "heat" on the street, Dick could have cared less.

The show's well-known director, Arthur Laurents, provided brief narration as Herman sat at his grand piano and engagingly performed six or seven songs from the score. Behind him was a huge bay window. Like many if not most auditions, this one had been scheduled for late afternoon. 4 o'clock. In early December. On a clear day. As Herman played, behind him the sun was setting over New York City.

Had there been a listing of credits for this presentation, it would have had to say, "Scenery and Lighting By God."

In the same way that many of Herman's shows conclude with a medley of reprises during curtain calls, so too did this audition end in a similar manner, reinforcing the melodic lines in the listeners' heads. By now it was dark outside, but to all of us inside Jerry Herman's townhouse there was the bright glow of a hit in the making. And Dick had entered his usual agitated state when *even he* knew something was good and that he had to compete with the Nederlanders and Shuberts.

Anyway, back to Clive, whom we left on hold several paragraphs ago.

"What did you think?" he asked of "La Cage."

"It can't miss" was my unhesitating response.

"That's what I think, too," he said, and then asked if I thought Jujamcyn and Arista should pursue it jointly for the St. James?

I responded that word on the street had it that Allan Carr, its lead producer, wanted the Palace.

"Allan's a friend of mine," Clive stated, "and I know he hasn't finalized anything yet."

I paused a moment to acknowledge to myself that *this* is the way top-level Broadway business gets done, and that I was now in the middle of it.

I told Clive that I needed to involve Dick at this point and told him to expect a call shortly to arrange a meeting. After thanking him, I hung up and immediately called Dick's assistant, Annette, telling her that I needed to see Dick right away. As she always did, Annette asked me idly, "Do you have a hit for us?"

This time I told her I actually might, then hurried out of the theatre and ran down Eighth Avenue to the St. James. On the way, I kept thinking with self-satisfaction that this opportunity and relationship I had created in less than four months on the job at Jujamcyn would have justified my salary for the whole year even if I had done nothing else.

When I arrived in Dick's office, he was in a foul humor and had a "This better be good" look on his face. I told him what had just happened with Clive.

"Does your friend Clive Davis have the money for the show?" he asked angrily.

"Not yet. He doesn't have the show yet. We have to create a partnership first to try to get Allan Carr to agree to do the show with us for the James."

"You know what?" Dick asked, as if I were wasting his time. "Tell your friend Clive Davis to come back to me with ninety percent of the money raised and I'll give him the final ten percent and a good theatre deal."

I couldn't believe what I was hearing. I tried to convince Dick that he needed to at least meet with Clive to discuss ways of proceeding in an alliance, but he only became angrier, saying things like "What? Ten percent isn't good enough for him?"

After about twenty minutes of this, I gave up. To say I was in a state of shock would be an understatement. He was flushing what could have been an incredibly beneficial relationship on the highest level right into the Broadway sewer system.

I called Clive back and made up some excuse along the lines that Dick, without my knowing it, had promised the St. James to a different show, and we had no other theatres that would work for "La Cage," but let's stay in touch.

I walked back to the Virginia and sat in my office in a state of total confusion and dismay. What had happened made no sense. On top of which, I felt helplessly isolated up here on 52nd Street in one of New York's colder theatres.

That would soon change, though. Dick would decide against building the development space he had hired me to oversee and instead provide more seed money for new projects for me to develop, which, in fact, I preferred. And the other denizens of the Virginia would soon depart as well, for Le G's "Alice in Wonderland" was a soporific that was hard to sit through, and it closed two weeks after its late December opening. Michelle would have to be content with going back to rolling in mud somewhere until her next show biz break came along.

The opening night of "Alice" had, though, provided me with one unexpected but memorable lesson. I always made sure that my friend John Rubinstein was included on Jujamcyn's invitation list for opening nights.

Three days before the opening of "Alice," John's father, the legendary pianist Arthur Rubinstein, died in Geneva, and John of course flew to Switzerland for his services. Discussing this with an office assistant, Sarah Linkoff (known later as the agent, Sarah Douglas), I told her to cancel his opening night tickets.

I was home in my apartment, changing for the opening late in the day on December 23rd, when my phone rang. It was Sarah. John had called from the airport to say that he had just returned from Europe and to confirm that his tickets were still set for that evening. She lied and told him they were, then called me in a panic. I told her to have the box office give him mine, and then to squeeze me in wherever they could. But talk about being stunned!

From that night on, I never took it upon myself to cancel anyone else's tickets, regardless of the circumstances.

Openin' Up the Ritz

Six months before I joined Jujamcyn in September, 1982, the big – and upsetting – news that dominated Broadway was the razing of two of Broadway's most desirable theatres, the Morosco on West 45th Street and the Helen Hayes, which abutted it on West 46th Street. Protests from a Who's Who of the theatre industry, led by Joseph Papp, had failed and the wrecking ball reduced them to a beautiful memory in order to create the space for a behemoth hotel designed by controversial Atlanta mega-developer John Portman.

Garnering much less industry attention and press coverage around the same time was Jujamcyn's acquisition and renovation of the 958-seat Ritz Theatre on West 48th Street, which had sporadically served as a legit house but for most of the prior 40 years had been used for a variety of different purposes ranging from a broadcast studio to a porn palace.

As I've previously noted, my first office with the company was located at the Ritz, where the renovation work was nearing completion. The only major question remaining on the table was whether to add one more row of seats at the rear of the orchestra, as Dick favored in order to increase the potential gross at capacity, or to leave enough room so patrons would have sufficient space to walk comfortably. After some internal debate, Dick decided to add the extra row of seats and – big surprise – on the rare occasions when the theatre was at or near capacity, the human traffic jams that resulted were as bad as the vehicular ones on the Long Island Expressway at rush hour.

Dick was intent on opening the refurbished Ritz with a play that would be looked upon as a prestigious booking, whether it was a huge success or not, and he wanted me to devote as much focus as I could to finding it. He was anxious to get a tenant, but he (rather wisely, I thought) also wanted to establish a strong aesthetic for the "new" theatre.

My first move was to get on a plane to Chicago, where a new play by Edward Albee, "The Man Who Had Three Arms," was being presented by the esteemed, not-for-profit Goodman Theatre. I was not alone in having a diminished opinion of Albee in the years since his intense 1962 drama "Who's Afraid of Virginia Woolf?" elevated him to the status of a – if not *the* – premier American dramatist.

After creating a highly charged, visceral experience for the theatregoer in "Virginia Woolf," it seemed he had often begun consciously trying to keep the audience at arm's length. His "A Delicate Balance" in 1966 had a coldness to its production that many (including my 16-year-old self) felt was off-putting; it wasn't until Gerry Gutierrez's stunning 1996 revival that the full emotional impact of the play was realized. The director of Albee's early plays was Alan Schneider, who was also a frequent director of Beckett, Brecht, and Pinter, and their influences became apparent in most of Albee's subsequent productions in the late '60s and '70s. Following "Balance" and the following year's "Everything in the Garden," Albee tended to indulge himself in the abstract or absurdist proclivities of those avant-garde writers, and audiences stayed away in droves.

However, I found myself pleasantly engaged by this latest effort of his, "The Man Who Had Three Arms." It was subsequently slammed by New York critics for being an exercise in self-pity or "a two-act temper tantrum," as Frank Rich described it in his *Times* review, but, for me, it was satisfying to be able to *feel* again at an Albee play. While it had an absurdist conceit at its center, it allowed for an emotional, not just intellectual, response. Was this enough to make it a Broadway hit? Probably not. But that wasn't my mission in coming to Chicago. I thought it could re-open the Ritz with class and respectability and not set the re-christened theatre on a course to be looked upon as a house of worthless flops.

Albee's agent was Esther Sherman, which made it easy for me to set a meeting with her and Albee in Dick's office. Esther arrived at the meeting totally frazzled.

"I'm going crazy, Stephen," she exclaimed in the outer office.

"Well, Esther, is it a good crazy or a bad crazy?" I inquired.

"I don't know, Stephen, I don't know," she manically bleated.

The meeting itself, though, went well. Albee was both receptive and appreciative. His one request was that, if he went with us, he wanted his longtime partners, Richard Barr and Charles Woodward, to be the lead producers. We were fine with that, and I agreed to meet with them to discuss the specifics.

Barr and Woodward insisted I meet them at their "other office," in a booth at the relatively new Restaurant Row brasserie and industry hangout, Mildred Pierce. Apparently, they lunched – and drank – there every day and even had a multi-line business phone on a chair right next to their booth. When I arrived, Barr picked up the handset and asked if I wanted to let my office know where I could be reached and he seemed disappointed when I told him my office already knew where I was.

Our lunch meeting was pleasant enough, if slightly strange, with both veteran producers drinking more than eating and Barr fielding a phone call or two and again asking if I wanted to check in with my office. If Jujamcyn was going to finance a large portion of the production, I wanted to make sure we were thinking of roughly the same capitalization and weekly budget numbers. I showed them a copy of some ballpark numbers I had run, including a hefty amount as a reserve and for advertising. And here's where the problem came in. They were under-budgeting, perhaps because they felt they couldn't raise their share of the amount that was truly needed; they had to know it would be even harder for them to entice investors this time given that the last several Albee plays on Broadway had been flops.

Perhaps it was the alcohol talking, but Barr took the position (and held to it) that "You don't need a reserve for an Edward Albee play."

Huh? I got the sense that they were romanticizing Albee's current stature, their minds stuck back in his "Virginia Woolf" days. Here I was in yet another situation where I was disagreeing with the industry veterans I had revered as a teenager. As awkward and disillusioning as it felt, I knew I was right, though.

I didn't fully realize it yet, but Dick was always looking for a reason *not* to proceed with a deal, and this, at first glance, gave him one of his more legitimate reasons for backing out. He could, however, have proceeded on the theory that Jujamcyn could lend the production additional capital on a "first out" basis if the investment of more money was warranted after its opening. In other words, take control of the situation, realizing that Jujamcyn, as the theatre owner, didn't stand to lose much regardless. Instead, he decided to bail and let Barr and Woodward fend for themselves. Interestingly, though, when the play was ultimately produced on Broadway the following April, opening at the Lyceum (a Shubert house), the only producer was Allen Klein, a major music industry mogul who had one Broadway credit to his name, a failed comedy he had produced in the spring of 1981. Barr and Woodward were nowhere to be found.

On the afternoon of the play's Broadway opening, I ran into Albee walking alone on Eighth Avenue. We chatted briefly and I wished him luck on his opening that night.

"It'll depend on whether the critics finally let me up or not," Albee responded.

They didn't, and "The Man Who Had Three Arms" closed after 16 performances.

I wasn't too sad that the Albee play had fallen through for Jujamcyn following my liquid lunch at "Mildred's." I had genuine enthusiasm for a different possibility. A new play by Lanford Wilson entitled "Angels Fall" had premiered at Circle Repertory Company that October and I saw it immediately at the invitation of Circle's managing director at the time, Richard Frankel. I was entranced by it. To this day, it's my favorite Wilson play.

The problem was a very mixed review by Rich in the *Times*. Could that be overcome? I felt it was worth a try, and, regardless, it would give Dick the prestigious opening attraction he wanted for the Ritz, which was supposedly the primary goal.

So we had another meeting in Dick's office, this time with Marshall W. Mason, who was Artistic Director of Circle Rep and the long-standing director of Wilson's plays. Marshall conveyed that Circle's board could commit to raising a third of the $300,000 cost of transferring the play to Broadway, as estimated by Frankel and me. Dick said Jujamcyn would also invest $100,000 if we could find the remaining third. This is one reason why Dick kept losing shows to the Shuberts, whose approach was to commit to doing a show and *then* finding partners if they wanted them. Dick was always hedging his bets, which I believe made prospective partners hesitant. In this case, it meant Marshall and me pounding the pavement.

I took an immediate liking to Marshall, who is one of the warmest and kindest people I ever met in my travels. He and I knocked on several doors but didn't make much progress. The lukewarm Rich review scared potential producing partners.

One of our outreaches was to veteran producer Claire Nichtern, who at the time was running the theatre division of Warner Brothers. She came to see the play one Saturday evening before its Circle Rep run ended and afterwards asked Marshall and me to meet with her in her Village apartment. It turned out to be a total waste of our time as she spent more than an hour and a half talking about everything except the play and its future. When we finally escaped, we went to a Village bistro for a 1 a.m. cheeseburger and acknowledged to each other that we were running out of both options and time.

What Marshall *didn't* acknowledge to me – and I in no way blame him for this – was that he was also pursuing a Shubert-anchored possibility, which eventually became reality with three producers in addition to the Shuberts. One of the producers was The Kennedy Center, whose chairman, Roger Stevens, Dick had a good relationship with and could just as easily reached out to, had he been so motivated. Dick, as I was learning though, wasn't a deal broker; he was more comfortable having a nearly completed deal come to him for a relatively modest investment and a "good theatre deal." It was a luxury that the president of one of the three Broadway theatre chains couldn't afford to have and effectively compete. I was cut out to do it, but I didn't have "President" next to my name.

The Shubert deal for "Angels Fall" came together rather quickly and the play opened on Broadway in January of 1983.

A few weeks prior, I received a call from Marshall inviting me to opening night and the party afterward and thanking me for all I had done to support his efforts. Usually, secretaries make this type of call, so it touched me that he reached out personally. Sadly, with only a few newspapers printing second reviews, "Angels Fall" landed quietly and, with word-of-mouth not doing the trick, shuttered after two months.

The next prospect, dubious as I thought it was, came to us. Martin Charnin asked for a meeting in Dick's office to discuss a new idea he had. With "Annie" well into its fifth year now, Marty had recently opened a successful revue in a cabaret in the theatre district whose name also served as the title of the revue: "Upstairs at O'Neal's."

Marty sat on the sofa in Dick's office and pitched his idea. It was for another revue, comprised of new talent and material, in something of a throwback to Leonard Sillman's "New Faces" series. He then went into a big windup to deliver the kicker and started laughing uncontrollably. "And you know what I'm calling it?"

No, tell us Marty.

"Crackers." And he cracks up again. "Get it. Crackers at the Ritz?" He truly thought it was the cleverest thing in the world. Dick smiled. I sat there stone-faced.

Anyway, Charnin had already hired Peter Neufeld as a general manager, and when Dick said he was interested, Marty arranged for Peter to meet with us to go over numbers to show how profitable it could be. The plan was that Marty and I would hold auditions for material over several days after the first of the year. I've never been a huge fan of the revue format, but scouting new talent with Charnin was the one and only aspect of the project that appealed to me, as I was always looking for opportunities to discover what new talent may be out there.

Another project crossed my radar that December, and this one was a missed opportunity.

The playwright and Emmy Award-winning television writer Lee Kalcheim had a new comedy called "Breakfast With Les and Bess" running at the non-profit Hudson Guild Theatre in Chelsea. Jujamcyn's eager new assistant literary manager saw one of its first performances and came back with a damning report that, like all of literary manager Barbara Laney's own written reports, was left on Dick's desk the following day. Dick always needed several people to agree with a positive internal report and reassure him, but a single negative one was all it took to scotch his interest. Thus, Frank Rich's subsequent positive review of the Kalcheim play in the *Times* wasn't enough to make him change his mind. So, being busy with my own development projects, I never saw it downtown.

In early 1983, though, the play did end up moving to the theatre district, but not to a Broadway contract house. It opened at the Lamb's, on 44th Street east of Broadway, in its beautiful 350-seat pecan-paneled theatre. It wasn't a full-fledged Broadway house, though, and that "neither/nor" status put constraints on "Les and Bess" both financially and competitively.

I would have jumped on it in a proverbial heartbeat for the Ritz, if only I had been the one from Jujamcyn to see it. The well-made Broadway comedy had become an endangered species, and Kalcheim had one here. Several years later, I worked with Lee on some network television concepts, and a close friendship evolved between our two families. Our one mutual regret was that we hadn't known each other back in the "Les and Bess" days, for, had I known Lee then, I would have been there before anyone else.

Meanwhile, over in "Crackers at the Ritz"-land, when the first of the year came, it was clear that auditions to find new talent would be delayed due to Charnin's schedule and that an opening couldn't happen that season. And as things played out, it never did happen. Charnin eventually did hold auditions at O'Neal's that spring, with me at his side, and he picked the writers/performers he wanted for this new revue. I thought he picked the best of the ones we saw, but I wasn't overwhelmed with any of them. Dick asked Marty to put together a presentation of the material at Sardi's Eugenia Room late one afternoon for potential producing partners. The highlight of the occasion for me was being able to re-affirm my conviction that Sardi's made the stiffest gin and tonics in New York. No one in attendance called Dick the next day to say "I'll die if I don't produce this revue with you," so he pulled the plug by nightfall.

But you're probably wondering if the newly renovated Ritz ever did manage to open that spring. There were no more "prestigious" options for me to present to Dick, but he knew it wouldn't look good to Binger if he couldn't open the theatre before the end of the season. So, after all I went through, he ended up booking The Flying Karamazov Brothers for a May 10th opening. After missing his opportunity on an Albee, a Wilson, and a Kalcheim, he ended up with a bunch of guys juggling toasters.

As proof that God works in mysterious ways, ten days before the toasters started flying at the Ritz, "My One and Only" had opened at the St. James, so Dick had a modest hit and a long-term tenant, and, for all I know, maybe he *did* think he had ended up with a prestigious opening attraction for the Ritz. In fact, if you took the Playbill at its word, the "Setting" of the action was "The stage of a prestigious Broadway theater."

Or at least one with air-conditioning that worked.

"We're Going to Make 'Marilyn' Fans Out of YOU!"

I was always amused by how producers who were new to Broadway, and who were often dilettantes, would be so persistent and annoying in pitching their shows, believing that their own enthusiasm would generate the same in us. And when that failed, they would sometimes resort to desperate ploys.

Some would come to me in hopes I'd take their show on as a development project in partnership with them, which I was wide open to doing if the concept and/or material "sang" to me. Some, though, just wouldn't take "no" for an answer and would keep finding ways of trying to sell me on it. There was one musical I must have passed on at least half a dozen times. But apparently that wasn't enough to get the message across. The "producer" got me on the phone somehow and haughtily said, "We're about to move on, but you're our first choice. I want to give you one final chance before it's too late."

Seriously?

I wished him luck. (His show never got on.)

Other times, the over-the-top enthusiast would be a neophyte producer whose show was capitalized and was looking for a theatre. I would sometimes sit in on these meetings with Dick.

On one such occasion, a general manager duo we knew and respected brought their producer-client in to pitch a musical about Marilyn Monroe that he was ready to bring to Broadway. Now. this dude was from another planet.

Actually, in the literal sense, not quite that far away. Only Australia. His opening salvo to us was an emphatic "We're going to make 'Marilyn' fans out of YOU!" He then told us about the worldwide search that was underway to find just the right person to play Marilyn.

Usually there's an exchange of dialogue in these types of meetings, but this fella was doing a non-stop sell. Dick and I could barely get a word in. I have always been a strong believer in letting the material sell itself, but what we had seen of it hadn't made us buyers.

He rambled on and on about how much of an icon Marilyn Monroe remains in American life today and, with the perfect casting he assured us would happen, how people would clamor to see a musical about her. And he kept returning to his insistent refrain: "We're going to make 'Marilyn' fans out of YOU!"

The guy was like a wind-up doll that kept going and going and never wound down. Feeling trapped in some sort of strange purgatory, I started thinking of ways we could put an end to his annoying pitch. Then fate intervened.

One of the guy's eyeballs fell out.

He quickly cupped his hand over his eye socket, having caught the eyeball with that hand as it started falling. The amazing part was that he kept right on pitching as if nothing had happened. Before long, though, he had to excuse himself and go put the glass eye back in.

It was hard to keep from laughing.

We seized the opportunity and ended the meeting with his general managers, who themselves were trying to stifle their laughter. Depending on his mood, Dick could be funny at times. Walking them out, he turned to them and delivered one of his better lines.

"Why don't you forget about searching for the perfect Marilyn and just put a wig on your producer?!"

A Viking Saga

Back in 1977 when Howard Ashman and I were working together on both "The Confirmation" and the launch of the WPA, he mentioned to Dennis Green and me an idea he had for a musical. At the time, Howard had a day job as an editorial assistant at Grosset & Dunlap. Part of his work there was editing the paperback compilations of *Hagar the Horrible* comic strips.

I was not familiar with *Hagar* at the time despite its popularity, but I soon became a fan of the cartoon Viking family that its author, Dik Browne, had created. Hagar, who made an honest living at ransacking and pillaging, and his long-suffering wife, Helga, were drawn in the comedy tradition of the Kramdens, Flintstones, and other couples with the blustery husband/impatient-but-loving wife dynamic. They were both on the hefty side physically, and they had two kids, a son named Hamlet who liked to (egad!) *read*, and a daughter, Honi, who had a mind of her own.

Ashman thought this would be ideal material for a musical and had even come up with the perfect casting: Zero Mostel and Barbara Cook. He quickly won me over and, since I was doing everything I could to find ways to help him financially while we prepped "The Confirmation" and the WPA, I paid him $500 to write a treatment.

I then made a play for the rights, which were owned by King Features Syndicate. Of course, we were both nobodies and didn't get very far, especially after their executive in charge mistakenly harbored an image of Barbara Cook from her pre-zaftig days and thus thought we misunderstood the character of Helga. So *Hagar* was put on the shelf.

I didn't forget it, though, and, when I joined Jujamcyn in September of 1982, trying again to secure the rights became a priority for me. Now I came dealing from strength, on top of which King Features had undergone a transformation and had a full-fledged entertainment division to deal with matters such as rights acquisition.

Jujamcyn opened its wallet, paid $10,000 up front to license the rights, as well as the customary gross and net participations, and we were set to go. Hey, maybe Dick Wolff was really serious about his commitment to developing shows.

I immediately sent Ashman a note, telling him I now had the rights and offering him the show he had once been eager to write. Of course, I still intended that Dennis would write the lyrics as the three of us had initially discussed five years prior, and maybe this played into Howard's disinterest since, in a backhanded slap, he had his assistant call me to say he was passing. I suspect his reason was a combination of not wanting to write a musical's book again without also doing the lyrics, his immediate commitment to direct subsequent productions of "Little Shop," and simply not wanting to work with me again. I've noticed throughout my career that it isn't unusual for artists to want to move beyond the peers they worked with in their early days and who helped them get their start, whether it's me or someone else. Chalk it up to human nature, I guess.

In truth, I was neither surprised nor overly saddened when Howard passed on it. And I had a clear conscience. Had I not offered the show to him, I would have felt I had stolen an idea that was his, regardless of whether I had commissioned a three-page treatment from him years before. This way, he might be frustrated that I had beaten him to the rights, but he couldn't say I had screwed him.

So now, where to turn? My first thought was Roger O. Hirson, the bookwriter of "Pippin," with whom I had had a good relationship working on an unsold tv series idea that I had developed with John Rubinstein. I described "Hagar" to Roger and he was interested. Given his "Pippin" credit – even if Fosse's final product did away with most of his original script – I knew I'd have no problem getting him approved by Dick.

The composer search was a bit more challenging, especially since we already had a lyricist, which instantly eliminated composers who served both functions or who had an established partner. We finally settled on Gary William Friedman, who was best known for having written a melodic score for a modest Broadway success, "The Me Nobody Knows," about a dozen years earlier.

Roger pitched me his "take" on the adaptation of the comic strip, and my main reaction was that "it isn't *Hagar*." He even mentioned to me that he saw an analogy between the Vikings and the I.R.A., which I totally didn't get. I tried to steer him more in the direction of the characters and sensibility of Dik Browne's strip. I could only hope he took it to heart.

He didn't. And Dennis and Gary's work followed suit. At one point I called one of their songs a "ditty" and Gary took offense. "Babe, I don't write ditties. I'm insulted you'd call something I wrote 'a ditty.'"

"Gary," I said, "it's a ditty and it's wrong for the show." Whatever one may think of Gary, you don't need to tiptoe around him.

It wasn't too long into the process that Roger withdrew from the project. I was never fully clear on his reasons, whether it was a professional conflict that had come up, or simply the sense that what he and the others were writing wasn't working and he didn't know how to change it.

At this point, Gary enthusiastically suggested we ask his friend Bob Randall to come aboard as librettist. We met with Bob and he was engaging and funny. He had been represented previously on Broadway by a semi-successful comedy called "6 Rms Riv Vu" and the hit musical "The Magic Show" (the success of which had all to do with magician Doug Henning and nothing to do with Bob's much-panned book). At the time, he was also showrunner on the hit television sitcom "Kate & Allie," although he would often be gratuitously catty in talking to us about its two stars, Jane Curtin and Susan St. James.

I saw the upside of hiring Randall, but I also sensed a potential downside, even if I couldn't really put the reason why into words. Dick and the others were gung-ho, though, so we brought him aboard.

Indeed, what Bob started churning out was funny – including a secondary character of his creation named Knut the Slovenly, a bedraggled Viking who lived in a shack and was romantically involved with a chicken. But, as with Hirson, it wasn't *Hagar*. Bob was imposing his own free creative choice on existing characters. And it all had a tawdry feel to it, with a huge helping of misogyny thrown in.

Dennis and Gary would write songs about whatever he told them to and were amused by what Bob was writing. All anyone could see was the funny, even when the book scenes went on forever and Bob wouldn't cut them. Meanwhile, believing as I do that there can be bad laughs as well as good laughs, my reservations kept mounting.

It was at about this juncture that Dick Wolff announced that Jim Binger would be in town from Minneapolis and they wanted to see a presentation of the material in Binger's apartment at the Sherry-Netherland. I felt I was losing control of this show, that it wasn't what I wanted it to be, but at least maybe if the Jujamcyn hierarchy saw it and shared my feelings, I could still right the ship.

Gary taught the score to a group of singers and rehearsed them until they had it nailed; they sold the music with professionalism and polish.

Arriving at Binger's apartment on the day of the presentation, everyone (of course) looked askance at the naked sailor woman mooning them as they entered the front hallway.

I introduced Bob, who narrated the presentation and a bit later sang one of the songs while grinding and exposing his belly button. That would have been nausea-inducing enough, but the song was called "Monogamy," which essentially summarized the philosophy Bob imposed on Hagar that "monogamy was never part of Mother Nature's plan/a single wife is not enough for any ordinary man," and went on to describe the menial chores women should do in order to please their men and masters.

Even though Dennis wrote the lyric at Bob's insistence, he cringed (and still does) at what came out of his pencil. As for me, I told all three of them I would never be in a theatre where it was performed because there was sure to be a riot.

Binger, however, loved it. Which meant that Dick, in turn, also loved it. And their love extended to the whole distorted show. Which meant I had a nightmare on my hands, especially when they both asked me how fast I could put a workshop together.

Now I was desperate, but I had one card left to play. We still didn't have a director, and there obviously couldn't be a workshop until we did. I had to think of a director who'd view the show in conceptual terms, not be scared off by its present state, and have the clout to insist on changes.

I asked Hal Prince if we could audition it for him, accepting that it was a work-in-progress. He graciously agreed, and Bob, Gary, and I gathered in his office to expose him to the show. Hal was in the most arid stretch of his career, having come off a string of failures and desperately needing a commercial hit. He took to the idea of a funny Viking musical immediately, clearly channeling his memories of "A Funny Thing Happened on the Way to the Forum," which he had produced two decades earlier. His initial reaction, however, was that the lyrics needed to be funnier (he hadn't actually read the book yet, but had laughed at several of the descriptions). He asked Dennis and Gary to go off and write three comedy songs, even if they didn't fit anywhere in the show. Gary amazingly balked a bit, asking if Hal really thought the existing songs weren't funny enough already.

"Look, it's just one man's opinion," Hal said.

To which, even more amazingly, Gary responded, "But what a man!"

I wanted the floor to open and swallow me whole.

Bob's relationship with Gary had already been showing signs of strain, with him at one point in recent weeks broaching the subject of bringing in a new composer to replace Gary. This was a move I was not about to make. And I heard plenty from Gary about Bob's attitude toward him: "Babe, can you believe this? After I was the one responsible for bringing him in."

Not a good idea, Gary, to remind me of that.

Regardless, Dennis and Gary did go off and write three comedy songs for Hal, and the two of them and I went back to Hal's office a few weeks later. Bob decided not to come since the reason for the meeting didn't involve him.

Dennis had outdone himself (as he would continue to do in writing funny and witty lyrics for the show), and Hal erupted into laughter several times as Gary performed them at the piano. Hal was now convinced of their ability to deliver and was ready to work on developing the show. I called Bob and left an effusive message on his answering machine, telling him about Hal's reaction.

Then, that night, Bob called Dennis and got *his* answering machine. The message he left was bizarrely unexpected, and Dennis kept the tape for his archives.

"I understand I'm not the hero anymore," he intoned in his lazy drawl. "I understand there's a new hero, a Dennis Something-or-other. Your message says I can talk for as long as I want, so I think I will."

And he droned on and on saying that he had decided to pull out of the show. He cited his personal differences with Gary and his sense that the show was now going in a direction he didn't like. But the sense we got was that he realized he wouldn't be the controlling force if Hal were involved, and his book would no longer be the dominant element of the project.

My reaction was one of relief, if not outright joy. My problem was solved. I would have another bite of the proverbial apple, and this time I was certain of how we could get the right bookwriter aboard and make the show work in a manner faithful to the original. As it happened, while the musical was going down the wrong track, I had come upon both the right story for the show and the writer to execute it.

I had left Jujamcyn as an employee by this point and was developing the show for them as an independent contractor, pocketing a fairly generous monthly fee (as I was on other ongoing projects I had put into development there as well). As a result of the relationship established on "Hagar," I had been hired as Head of Creative Affairs for King Features Entertainment, where one of my duties was to produce prime-time animated specials for CBS based on noted comic strips owned by KFE's parent Syndicate.

One of those was *Hagar the Horrible*. While interviewing writers in Los Angeles, I met and struck up an instant rapport with a young comedy writer named Douglas Wyman. We were on the exact same wavelength about what "Hagar" should be, so I hired him and we started. We found the key to making the franchise viable, and Doug wrote a 23-minute script that was funny and ultimately poignant and, most important, true to Dik Browne's characters. CBS loved it and we were green-lighted to production, for which Hanna-Barbera would be the animation company working with us.

When I hired Doug, he was a writer on the *Newhart* sitcom for CBS; soon afterward he was promoted to being its showrunner/ Executive Producer and quickly became one of the hottest comedy writers in Hollywood. Add to this that we loved working together and he loved the *Hagar* franchise, and my first move after Randall quit the musical became a no-brainer. Only problem was that, sought after as Doug was in television, I knew Dick would object to hiring him because he didn't have any Broad-WAAAY experience.

So I called Hal and asked him to trust me on this and try to convince Dick to go along. To my lasting appreciation, Hal didn't hesitate. Hearing that Hal endorsed Doug's hiring was all Dick needed to approve it.

Finally, we were off and running in the right direction. Doug and I continued to work closely and make creative decisions together and feed song ideas to Dennis. Not much of what had been written by Dennis and Gary before could be salvaged.

And with Hal involved, there'd be no more ridiculous exercises such as Dick interfering for one brief, un-shining moment to "suggest" that Gary and Dennis write a big, traditional Broad-WAAAY number for the show, maybe a rousing title song, which at one point they had done at his insistence. The result would only qualify as bad parody.

Of course, Dick liked it because he thought it would be an audience-pleaser. "You know what business I'm in?" he asked Gary rhetorically. "I'm in the *tuchus* business. My job is putting *tuchuses* in seats."

"I'm hip, babe, I'm hip," Gary replied.

Bless you, Hal, for rescuing me.

Hal's favorite way of communicating new ideas was through short notes to me that would arrive in the mail. The theme of the show was Hagar and the Viking world trying to fight off the encroaching forces of civilization, so an example of the type of note Hal would send me was "What if the invading forces are French? The French are funny. Tell the fellas. Hal"

His mantra was to go broad and broader. Be as outrageous as possible within the confines of the conceit.

He also rejected one of the early musical numbers with the simple question to me, "How am I supposed to stage this?" He stressed that in the conception of any given number, we needed to always keep in mind what should be happening on stage during it. In this and other instances, Hal made me better. To use a tennis analogy in regard to my skill at developing musicals, by this point in my career I could reliably hit the ball over the net with authority. Hal taught me how to put spin on it.

It didn't take long for a first draft of the script to be completed, as well as many of the songs. Hal wanted to arrange a reading, but only of the first act because he felt the second act didn't work yet. I wasn't satisfied with it myself, but the solution had been evading both Doug and me. As for the first act, it was everything I had always wanted it to be.

Hal asked if we could do the reading on the stage of the St. James Theatre one morning, and it was a request easily granted. Then he began casting the reading, often calling me to discuss options. He particularly wanted my opinion of whether his daughter, Daisy, would be a good choice as Hagar's daughter, Honi, to read opposite Harry Groener as her French suitor. I said fine, and she and Groener made a funny and endearing pair of young comic lovers. My strongest memory of Groener, though, was when the action didn't involve his character; he had a smile of genuine enjoyment on his face throughout the reading, the memory of which would give me reassurance for months any time I had doubts.

Hal had very few notes afterwards; it was clear to him, as it was to us all, that the first act worked liked gangbusters. He just wanted us to keep going broader, add more musical "fragments" where we could, and – the biggie – solve the second act while he was in London directing "Phantom of the Opera," after which we'd regroup and discuss next steps.

No matter what plot machinations we tried in the second act, though, it seemed flat after what we had given the audience in the first. By the time "Phantom" opened in the West End, we were still struggling to find an answer.

As Doug was based in southern California, with limited time because of *Newhart* and having a strong aversion to airplanes, I finally decided the rest of us had to pick a week he wasn't in production and fly out there. Somehow I got Jujamcyn to agree to foot the bill for a handful of rooms at a resort in Indian Wells, a desert oasis away from the distractions of L.A. where we could all be together and focus intently on the second act.

It worked. I became convinced that our problem wouldn't be solved until we found a way of playing out the story that went beyond plotting and basic character. After a few days, it came to us. It had to do with varying the perspective, and once we knew the conceit, everything else fell into place right away. We left the desert knowing we had it licked.

The second act was almost fully completed in a matter of months, and the process went without a hitch now that we had a road map we knew was reliable. I sent it over to Hal, who was now in the process of prepping and casting the Broadway production of "Phantom."

Ironically, something else happened at this juncture. Dennis' close friend, the late Broadway musical director Eddie Strauss, who had always been a fan of the project, asked to read the finished product. Dennis gave it to him, thinking nothing of it. But, Eddie, being suitably impressed, gave it to Jerry Zaks, with whom he was working on the Lincoln Center revival of "Anything Goes."

Next thing we know, Eddie's telling Dennis that Zaks thinks it's terrific and might want to consider directing it. I've always found it curious that two of the top directors of the era sparked to the project when other second-rung directors who had read it at various points hadn't.

Suddenly, we had *two* enviable options.

But not for long.

Annette Meyers, Hal's longtime assistant, called and said Hal would like to meet with me in his office. It turned out, in a strange way, to be the warmest meeting I ever had with him. He was effusive about the work we had done.

"You guys have done everything I asked of you," he said. "This show could run two years and win several Tonys," he continued. Then came what I least expected. "But you'd be short-changing yourselves," he added.

Short-change us, Hal. Please short-change us, I thought.

"Now that you've made it broad and funny, you need to make it *important*."

I was perplexed. I had no idea what he was talking about, and he could see my confusion.

"Don't you think the comic strip is *significant?*" he asked.

"I think it's Ralph and Alice in Viking horns," I answered.

We had a somewhat lengthy conversation in which I struggled to grasp how he would envision this overlay of "significance" working. He wasn't sure and wanted us to think about it. I said we would, but I was honest in expressing my skepticism that we would be able to meet this challenge. It sounded like he was talking about a totally different show than what he had been envisioning before "Phantom" became a mega-hit. And I didn't want it to be a different show.

Hal couldn't have been friendlier, but he made it clear that he wouldn't be interested in directing if we couldn't "take it to the next level." He said he'd understand if we didn't want to travel down this road and that there were directors of pure comedy who'd be attracted to the property as it stood, ironically adding "like Jerry Zaks."

I left Hal's office that day knowing we'd be proceeding without him. He hadn't directed a lighthearted show in over two decades, and, after "Phantom" had revived his career, he didn't need to now. "The fellas" and I did try to figure out what he meant by "make it important," but the image we kept conjuring was that of Norse gods observing the cartoon Vikings from above and cackling at their human foibles. It was an image that was so bad it made us want to throw up, but it was the one that stuck in our minds.

With Hal now out of the picture, I arranged a meeting with Jerry Zaks at Joe Allen. He was obviously smitten with the show but wasn't prepared to commit yet. At this juncture, I needed a commitment.

Meanwhile, there was a sea change occurring at Jujamcyn. Jim Binger had hired Rocco Landesman to take over for Dick Wolff. It was a smart move. I knew and liked Rocco from our involvement together on a commission comprised of young producers looking at possible ways of reducing Broadway costs. Before he formally assumed the presidency of Jujamcyn, he asked to meet with me to get my thoughts on the operation, during which he was curious if I thought that Jack Viertel would be a good choice to fill my former position. I did, and Rocco told me he was in the process of hiring him. Even though Rocco wanted to hear the projects I had been working on as an independent contractor, I knew Jack would want to start with a clean slate. (In that meeting, I also sang the praises of Howard Rogut, whom he likewise admired, and suggested that he fire Aldo Scrofani, which he didn't want to consider at that time because he felt he needed to maintain continuity. But, in due course, Aldo was out and Paul Libin joined the team.)

Jujamcyn wouldn't be renewing the rights to "Hagar" or, obviously, continuing payments to me. By now I was firmly ensconced at King Features, making a transition into television, so I didn't need the money. And I could still play the last card in my deck on "Hagar" because I happened to be a creative executive with the company that controlled the underlying rights.

Some months earlier, I had sent the "Hagar" script to my good friend Kary Walker, who was Producing Director at Marriott's Lincolnshire Theatre outside Chicago. I had seen several shows there and had been impressed with their quality. After reading the script, Kary called me, exclaiming in his inimitable way, "I laughed out loud! I *don't* laugh out loud." He said he wanted to consider it for production.

His enthusiasm grew and before long I found myself in Lincolnshire, ironically at the same time as Marriott's theatre attorney and our mutual friend, Marsha Brooks, who at the time was with the prestigious Colton, Weissberg firm. We all wanted to see a Larry Shue comedy that was playing at Milwaukee Rep, so the three of us drove up there one night and on the way back in Kary's car began good-natured negotiations for a "Hagar" production at Lincolnshire, breaking into frequent laughter as Marsha determinedly tried to take notes in the dark.

Soon afterwards, Kary called me and suggested we do a reading of the show on the Lincolnshire stage. I, of course, immediately agreed. Kary and his Artistic Director, Dyanne Earley, then put together a cast comprised of Chicago actors, and Dennis, Gary, and I flew out for a long weekend of rehearsals, with most of that time devoted to the music. Again, poor Doug was stuck in L.A.

There was an invited audience of about a hundred people on hand for the reading. For these occasions, Kary always handed out comment cards for the audience members to fill out and hand back. He warned us beforehand not to be discouraged by how negative they usually were.

The reading itself fulfilled our expectations of the show, even if some of the actors were wrong for their parts or made bad acting choices. The humor shone through, and, most importantly for us because we had never seen it performed before, the second act worked just as we had hoped.

Still, when Kary handed us the audience comment cards, he again warned us to brace ourselves. (Personally, as with Howard Ashman a decade earlier in Princeton, I trusted my own instincts enough that I really didn't care what they said.) But as we read them one by one, we were shocked.

They were almost all positive, enthusiastic, and complimentary. Not what we had been led to expect, but a nice surprise.

No Chicago production materialized, however. Kary never gave me a specific reason, but my educated guess has always been that his Artistic Director wasn't a fan. In fact, after the reading, I happened to hear a companion of hers begging her not to do it. Whether there was an agenda at play or she just sincerely didn't take to the material is anybody's guess. But, if this *is* what happened, I appreciate the handcuffed position it put Kary in.

With no producing entity and no director, and me being increasingly consumed by television work, the time had come to back-burner the project, maybe for good. Over the years, Gary Friedman has come to me a few times with either a small theatre company that's interested or a journeyman director who'd like to do a reading of the show, and every time I've expressed no interest. For one thing, we no longer have the rights and I'm long gone from King Features (which is now known as Hearst Entertainment), as are most of the people in charge when I was there. To open that Pandora's box again, knowing the ultra-conservative mentality of the Hearst Corporation board, I knew I'd need a solid, first-class package. And I also knew that's what I'd need in order for the show to be a success.

In retrospect, one missed opportunity I do regret was not giving the material to a young choreographer I hired for a television project in the early '90s, who was a joy to work with, showed directorial prowess as well, and would have been a perfect sensibility match. But it never even occurred to me back then to broach the subject to Jerry Mitchell, probably because in those days attaching him to it would have had as little impact as Ashman's involvement had had when I first went after the rights in 1977.

Regardless, I am fulfilled by a certain posthumous kinship I feel with Howard. I know he would be impressed by what we ultimately created out of his idea, despite all the detours. And I think he'd be pleased that I didn't compromise just to get an inferior production or reading of the show done. I'd much rather live with my vision of the terrific show it could be than the memory of third-rate talents having bastardized it. I'm proud we were finally able to create the show on paper that Howard, Dennis, and I had initially envisioned, and that at least it remains untarnished. Sure better than having it sacked and pillaged.

The Case of the Missing Usherettes

Scams are perpetrated regularly on Broadway. Always have been, always will be. Most occur in and around the box office of hit shows. But some are carried out in places you'd never suspect.

An older gentleman named John Larsen was house manager of the Virginia Theatre when the revival of "On Your Toes" starring famed Russian ballerina Natalia Makarova played 505 performances there starting in March of 1983.

Larsen took his job seriously and while people may have mistaken his quiet demeanor for obliviousness to what was going on around him, he was actually very alert and observant. One night just before the doors opened to let the audience in, he noticed that there seemed to be fewer usherettes than usual in the house.

For the next several performances, he made a point of counting usherettes and at each performance he discovered that there were several fewer than the theatre had contracted for. Probably just a coincidence that several were out sick at the same time.

The following week he counted again. Same shortage. Except, he realized, for one small difference. The usherettes who had been out the prior week were now back and it was *others* who were missing.

He started asking questions and soon enough he uncovered the truth: the head usherette, who resembled a female Jimmy Cagney and held one of the top positions in their union (yup, even usherettes have a union), was forcing a handful of her colleagues each week to take some time off and sign their paychecks over to her. (The time off may have been the carrot that made the scam work...who knows.) If they didn't, she had ways of making them regret it.

Basically, Jujamcyn was getting ripped off, which, in turn, meant the production was getting ripped off since the costs of theatre personnel (and every other conceivable thing, as well as some inconceivable ones) get passed along. To explain how this works, when funds from ticket sales come in, they go to the theatre, not the production, and at the end of every week of a show's run, the theatre deducts the week's rent and operating expenses (usually inflated) from the gross box office receipts attributable to that performance week and then forks over the remainder to the production. The show that people are buying tickets to doesn't see the money from sales until then, nor does it typically receive the interest that the money from advance sales earns.

Dick and Aldo were none too happy when Larsen brought this scam to their attention, for it meant they'd at least have to have a meeting with the Cagney look-alike and her sister, who was also some sort of muckety-muck in the usherette's union. Howard Rogut had told me that the sisters didn't get along and, from the sound of things in Dick's office, they were even at each other's throats during this meeting. Yet, from what I gathered afterwards, it seemed to me that Dick was less annoyed with them for perpetrating the scam than with Larsen for uncovering it and creating an unnecessary problem for him to have to deal with. Unbelievable.

But then, usherettes scamming? Pretty unbelievable itself.

And Some People Think It's Easy

The naked guys first exposed themselves to me on the Long Island Railroad.

A bit of background is necessary. A few months after I joined Jujamcyn, I arrived at Joe Allen one day for a meeting with Roger O. Hirson, in fact the one at which I presented my nascent "Hagar" project to him in the hope it might appeal to him as a librettist. Roger was just wrapping up a prior meeting about a new play of his with a young director out of Harvard named Andy Cadiff. Cadiff and I chatted for a few minutes before he departed, during which time he asked me if I'd be willing to read the script and listen to a tape of a new musical he was working on. I said I would; in my new position, that response was automatic.

But I did have the choice of putting it on the pile of unread scripts in my office, and that's exactly what I did. Sooner or later I'd get to it. Since the overwhelming numbers of unsolicited scripts, readings, workshops, and out-of-town productions that vied for our attention were almost always disappointing and had little-to-no potential, evaluating them was usually an exercise in tedium and frustration.

A few months later, though, as I left for a dentist appointment on Long Island, I grabbed the script and cassette that Cadiff had given me. On the train ride back to the city, I stuck the cassette in my Walkman and began listening half-heartedly to the score. About three songs in, I realized I needed to start paying closer attention. When I got to the sixth and final song on the demo tape – a chillingly beautiful ballad about the disillusionment of my generation called "I Don't Believe in Heroes Anymore" – I realized the material was striking a profound societal chord that spoke to me with the immediacy of our time. I then replayed the entire cassette.

By the time the train pulled into Penn Station, I knew I wanted to produce this show.

I hadn't read a word of the script, but, heck, whatever might be wrong with it, we could fix. There was way too much quality and contemporary sensibility in the six songs I heard to simply walk away.

I was aware there was a looming problem, though. My mission at Jujamcyn was to develop shows that might eventually play in one of their five Broadway theatres, and a three-character musical with the title "3 Guys Naked from the Waist Down" had the decided "feel" of belonging off-Broadway. Still, it was the most exciting musical project I had come across, and I couldn't get it out of my mind.

As I wrestled with the dilemma, I began talking to Cadiff more about his vision for it and eventually met the two creators, Jerry Colker and Michael Rupert. They had initially come up with the idea of a musical about stand-up comics while acting together in "Pippin" on Broadway, had written the first of many, many drafts, and then brought Cadiff on board to work with them. I wasn't familiar with Colker but had admired Rupert's work as an actor dating back to when I first saw him perform in the Kander-Ebb musical "The Happy Time" in early 1968. I had no idea, though, that he was as talented a composer as he was an actor.

At some point that fall, I gave the cassette of the score to Max Weitzenhoffer, a wealthy art gallery owner and Broadway producer friend of Dick's whom I was just getting to know. Max fell in love with the score and expressed interest. He shared the cassette with his and Dick's toy executive friend, Ray Larsen, who had been an investor/associate producer in numerous McCann-Nugent productions on Broadway. Ray also responded positively. Like Max,

Ray was as kind a soul as ever was involved in producing, and I came to treasure our budding friendship.

Not insignificantly, this also solved my Jujamcyn problem. Dick always liked reassurance, and Max and Ray wanting to partner on "3 Guys" was the security blanket he needed to green light it. We further told him that if it was received well off-Broadway, it could possibly move to the Ritz, given that theatre's small size.

So we set about putting together a workshop production. Casting the show was a huge challenge even though it only had three characters. All three actors had to have stand-up comedy skills. And be able to sing, act, and move well. The most challenging role to fill was that of the disturbed conceptual comic, Kenny. We auditioned so many young actors and comics that my ever-loyal casting director, Leonard Finger, became exasperated. (What I loved about working with Leonard was that he was both a witty character and a dapper throwback to an earlier era. Just walking into his office overlooking Times Square and seeing him sunk in his chair behind an oversized desk, with a pocket square in his jacket, was like being transported back to Damon Runyon's Broadway. So when he became exasperated, it would come off as funny.)

But it *was* reaching the point that Cadiff and Colker had to settle on *somebody* if the show was ever going to go into rehearsal. At the last minute before a compromise decision was made, The Finger stumbled upon an extraordinary young guy doing street comedy outside the Metropolitan Museum of Art and invited him to audition.

John Kassir was fresh, wildly inventive, and hysterically funny. He wasn't an actor, but his acting was passable. The problem was his singing, but Rupert told me it could be improved if I were willing to authorize as a production expense weekly lessons from a top vocal coach he himself had worked with. I was, and Kassir continued going to that teacher on our coin for over a year while the show was in gestation. (It paid off.)

We rented one of the small theatres on Theatre Row and the workshop got under way. I would get daily reports of the progress, but I pretty much left the creative team alone. Four weeks later we had several run-throughs for invited audiences. I knew the show still had problems, but the audiences would be friends of people connected with the show.

What I didn't know was that Jerry Colker had told his and Cadiff's William Morris agent (the wonderful Dan Mizell, who died at far too young an age) to invite folks. So imagine my shock when I entered the theatre for the first "performance" only to see the entire William Morris theatre department lined up in the back row. And a who's who of Broadway insiders in many of the other 80 or so seats.

What happened then wasn't pretty. The show was overlong, the laughter was minimal, and even Kassir's sure-fire first act routine played poorly. It was so agonizing that when I walked into the lobby to escape for a few minutes, I saw Rupert stretched out on a bench, visibly trembling.

I suggested we get out of there before people came out for intermission. He shakily agreed. On the sidewalk, we realized that the inevitable walkouts would head to the nearby upscale watering holes, so, wanting to avoid them, we headed to The Blarney Stone, a block away on the other side of 42nd Street. Soon after taking our seats at the bar, I turned toward the door and was momentarily startled.

"What?" Rupe asked, nervously.

"For a second I thought I saw Kassir coming in," I replied.

"My God!" he said, panicked, "It's so bad the actors have left!"

The remaining invited audiences proved more encouraging. But by that point in the workshop, we knew a lot of work still needed to be done. One problem we had already reached agreement on: to cut a rousing, audience-pleasing number in the middle of the second act called "Mediocrity." Once it had been sung, the remainder of the show sank; the audience lost interest in the three guys they had grown attached to in the first act because after performing that number they were coming across as disingenuous and hypocritical. A textbook lesson in musical theatre construction: sometimes material doesn't work because of something that comes before, no matter how good that something is on its own.

We opted to plan a second workshop, this time in a rehearsal space instead of a small theatre. Cadiff and Colker continued working together on the script throughout the intervening months; Jerry was hardly the most willing writer to cut material he had written that he loved, so this was an often-torturous process.

We also decided we needed to recast the role of Ted, the ingratiating emcee comic, with an actor the audience would instantly take to. Enter Scott Bakula. To this day, "Baksy" (he calls me "Wellsy") remains the one actor who could always make me smile, just upon seeing him, largely because he was a genuinely nice guy with a positive attitude who never made waves. Adding his talent and spirit to the chemistry of the show was one of the smartest decisions we made, and he fit in perfectly with Kassir and Anthony Crivello, who played the "angry guy" comic.

The show got better and better in the second workshop, especially after we were able to get Jerry to agree to cut an embarrassingly ineffective number in the first act called "Poppa." And this time we controlled the guest list better.

We now needed to get "3 Guys" to a stage somewhere prior to New York. Aside from the fact that the show needed to play before a real audience prior to New York, Dick was, as usual, anxious to have a "cheap look-see" before further committing or, more likely I knew by then, finding a reason not to. I began exploring possibilities with regional theatres that might be interested in both the show and our enhancement money.

I thought that Chicago, given the reputation it enjoyed as home of Second City and other comedy troupes, would be the ideal place to launch "3 Guys Naked." Soon after I joined Jujamcyn in the fall of 1982, I had seen Dorothy Loudon in a one-woman comedy at an off-Loop theatre in Chicago named Wisdom Bridge, and had met its managing director, Jeff Ortman.

I called Ortman, told him about the project, and asked if I could send the script and cassette of the score to him for his and Artistic Director Bob Falls' review. It didn't take long for him to get back to me expressing interest in including our show in their coming season. We continued to discuss arrangements, including reasonable enhancement money from us, and everything fell into place much more smoothly than usually happens. (It helps when the person you're negotiating with is sane and knowledgeable; not always the case.)

However, there was one "formality" he asked if we'd accommodate before it was all set in stone. Falls wanted to meet our creative team. It was a reasonable request, and since we already knew they wanted to do the show, I agreed to fly Falls and Ortman to New York for one day to accomplish this. And so, on Memorial Day, 1984, we all gathered in Andy Cadiff's Manhattan Plaza apartment. The three actors joined Cadiff, the two writers, and me for the first hour of the meeting and it was a lovefest.

Then, soon afterwards, as the rest of us were talking, Cadiff casually mentioned to Falls that he had just been hired to direct an off-Broadway play called "Losing It" that would be scheduled so as not to conflict with Wisdom Bridge's "3 Guys" dates. It had tried out in Chicago and he wondered if Falls had heard about it or possibly even seen it.

An awkward silence ensued. Finally, Falls said, "I directed it."

Instantly, the temperature in the room dropped substantially.

Falls hadn't been retained for the New York production of this (forgettable) play and had been replaced by the director he was on the verge of inviting to work at his home theatre.

The meeting became perfunctory from then on. Nothing was acknowledged, but the inevitable outcome was palpable in the air, if unspoken. The "second city" syndrome had reared its head.

The next day, Ortman, back in Chicago, called me and apologized, saying how embarrassed he was. He didn't agree with Falls' reaction, but he obviously had to abide by what his Artistic Director had decided, whatever his reason.

So where to turn now? I scoured my Rolodex for contacts I had in regional theatres, and I realized that Bob Tolan, whom I had gotten to know when he was Producing Director of the Virginia Stage Company in Norfolk, was now at Playmakers Rep in Chapel Hill, North Carolina. I called Bob and he was interested. One thing quickly led to another, and we secured a deal for a three-week run at their theatre on the University of North Carolina campus in September, outside of their regular season, on basically a "four-wall" arrangement. Running the numbers, I realized we needed to come up with $45,000 in advance capitalization to make this happen and to absorb any potential losses. Even though that was much more than what our commitment would have been as part of Wisdom Bridge's regular season, with the high-powered money people we were working with, that amount shouldn't be a problem, I thought.

But I thought wrong.

Dick called a meeting in his office of all the principals – Dick, me, Max, Ray, and Cadiff. He also had his attorney, Seth Shapiro, present, which was unfortunate, not because he was a lawyer but because he was a former producer. It soon became apparent that Seth had convinced Dick that the show needed a gag writer, and Seth knew just the person from Hollywood to bring in. Dick conditioned Jujamcyn's continuation with the project on Cadiff and me agreeing to this course of action.

We refused. And the meeting got testy. Cadiff later told me that Dick must like me a lot because he didn't fire me for openly defying him. But, in the room, Dick had numbers on his side. He convinced Ray to go along with him. At least I knew I had Max I could count on. Until I didn't. He quietly followed the lead of his two friends.

Neither Cadiff nor I took our stand simply out of loyalty to Jerry Colker. Above all, the show didn't need a "gag writer," and, regardless, you don't just call in a "punch-up guy" on an avant-garde concept musical. Of course, this type of thinking eluded Dick.

The bottom line is that we left the meeting with Jujamcyn still holding the rights to the show but putting it in cold storage. Nothing more could happen with it.

Cadiff called Colker and had him meet us on the patio at Curtain Up, the restaurant that at the time was on the ground floor of Manhattan Plaza. Colker saw a phone booth on the corner and went to call Dick, Ray, and Max at each of their homes. Amazingly, he got each of them to call him back when his first three minutes were up and the operator wanted more money. (Things were so different before cell phones!) He returned to the table briefly after speaking to Dick and told us nothing had changed but he felt better. We asked him why.

"I told him, 'Fuck you, Dick.'"

We then asked what Dick had said.

"He said, 'Fuck you, Jerry.'"

A constructive exchange, to be sure.

During Jerry's conversation with Max, he motioned to me to come over, and when I got there he said Max wanted to talk to me.

"You're going to get yourself fired, you know," Max told me.

"I don't care, Max! I'm going crazy in this nuthouse!" I responded.

"Well," Max said in his Oklahoma drawl, "I'm sure you're going to continue to try to get the show to Chapel Hill, and I just want you to know you can count on me for at least $10,000. But Dick can't know."

Now I really was going crazy. Two hours ago he had pulled out of the show. Now he was back in…albeit secretly. But the one thing it did was give me hope that we could find a way to salvage the show and the tryout.

As midnight approached and Cadiff, Colker, and I were still sitting at the table, I came up with an idea. I knew I had to somehow wrest the rights away from Dick, but since I was an employee of his, he had to think I had nothing to do with it. I needed to find a producer to partner with, and I remembered that Jim Freydberg, whom I'd gotten to know when he produced "Baby" the prior year, had come to the second workshop and been a fan…even if he had appeared to be in agony as he watched it. (Lesson: Never try to interpret someone's physical response.)

But before we did anything, we had to see if the actors were still with us. We had told them they'd be signing an off-Broadway contract at the same time as the Chapel Hill one, but with Jujamcyn and Ray now out, and Max functioning surreptitiously, they'd have to roll the proverbial dice along with us. Bakula was my first call the next morning, and he didn't hesitate; he believed in the show and was ready to invest more of his time and talent. Kassir was also quick to agree.

Tony Crivello proved the problem, but primarily because his agent had already been trying to talk him out of leaving Manhattan for three weeks during prime casting season. He withdrew, maybe thinking we'd come back to him if we did make it to New York following the tryout. But with the more critical two of the three saying yes, we pushed forward. We'd recast the angry guy comic.

I then called Freydberg and asked if I could meet with him that afternoon. I had Cadiff come with me and we outlined the situation to him. I told him that if he came aboard and could wrest the rights from Dick, I'd take responsibility for finding the $45,000 we needed for the tryout, partner with him on the sly for now, then openly afterwards. Other than Max's $10,000, I wasn't sure how I'd find the rest of the funds as quickly as we needed to, but I had to remove any excuse Jim might have for not committing.

The strategy worked. Freydberg called Dick and got him to agree to sign over the rights, but with one condition: that Jim agree to give him first refusal on booking it into a Jujamcyn theatre if it ever came to Broadway. Vintage Dick...he had ceased believing in the show, but wanted to hedge his bets; truth is, he never knew what he believed in. Freydberg and I both wanted the show to have a clean break from Jujamcyn, but we didn't have much choice at this juncture, so we agreed to it.

It turned out to be easier than I thought for me to put the try-out financing together, with my good friend and marketing expert Mike DeLuise kindly introducing me to an investor who put up the final significant chunk of it.

I started spending a few hours of each day in Freydberg's office, which was full of positive energy. In many ways, Jim was the best producer I ever worked with, except when his explosive temper made him sometimes hard to tolerate. He also had the unbecoming habit of trashing people behind their backs. One day following a meeting with my beloved accountant, Bernie Rosenberg, that I had to depart from early, Bernie called me to say the minute I had left the room, Jim started bad-mouthing me. I laughed and told him Jim did that to almost everybody. But when it came to the nuts-and-bolts of putting a show together, he was terrific to work with.

We began a brief rehearsal period in a space at the Puerto Rican Traveling Theater Company on West 47th Street. Unfortunately, the actor we had hired to replace Crivello turned out to be *too* much of an angry guy – at one rehearsal, he threw an ax into the rehearsal floor – and we had to make another casting change. With little time remaining before we left for Chapel Hill, our best option seemed to be installing Colker into the role since he was a professional actor and had based the character on himself. So that's what we did.

On Labor Day, we lit out for North Carolina. The theatre's tech director was a native Carolinian named Linwood, and what I most remember of the tech period is him continually telling me "You better get them Wallaces." I had no idea who the Wallaces were, but I wasn't about to hire them or anybody else. Finally, Cadiff informed me that what Linwood was trying to tell me through his thick Southern accent was that we needed "wirelesses." Microphones. And Cadiff was agreeing with him. I approved the expense.

My one hesitation about taking "3 Guys" to Chapel Hill was whether a rural audience – which is what we'd draw other than members of the university community – would relate to the show's more urban sensibility. I needn't have worried. They got it. And they embraced us. We toyed with the show for the first two performance weeks, making adjustments based on how material played.

These were without question the best three weeks of my professional life. We all knew we were working on something special, the chief critic in the Triangle area gave us a near-rave, and audiences were responding more and more positively each week. The company – myself included – stayed at a simple motel on the outskirts of town. Many nights, our orchestrator, Michael Starobin, would drop by my room, plop himself in a chair, and talk for fifteen minutes. One night, just before he was supposed to leave for New York to do orchestrations for a Public Theater production, he came into my room and literally begged me to let him stay for the rest of our run and continue to play the show, saying he could do his work for Joe Papp from here. He even said he'd pay his own expenses. Of course, I told him yes, he could stay, but no, he would *not* be allowed to pay for anything. At the time, Starobin was viewed as the most sought-after young talent in his profession.

The humor of the run was provided by our New York press agent, Jeff Richards, who flew into town for a few days with a mission to demonstrate to his local counterparts how to pull out all the stops in aggressively promoting a show. In a funny clash of cultures, he'd run in front of a bus on Franklin Street, wave his arms for it to stop, get in the front door, hand flyers to all the bewildered passengers, and then exit through the rear door, all in a matter of seconds. Bicyclists wouldn't stop for Jeff, so he'd just hand them flyers as they sped by. And he'd create special, unauthorized ticket discounts as he saw fit, creating chaos for the box office manager.

More from the enthusiastic word-of-mouth than from Jeff's manic blitz, by our final week in Chapel Hill we began to sell out. I had taken accumulated vacation days to be away from Jujamcyn for this stretch, but it ceased to be a secret where I was or what I was doing. I had decided I'd be leaving Jujamcyn when I got back from Carolina, but I thought there was more to be gained by keeping everything friendly and respectful.

Dick had seen the reviews of the tryout and was now afraid he was missing out on something. So on the final Thursday of the run, he and his wife, Fran, along with Max and his wife, Fran, flew down to see that evening's performance.

We were all psyched, feeling we had a point to make, and the show came through for us. It played better than ever. Laughter and applause throughout. And, at the end, a spontaneous standing ovation. I felt a high similar to that night in Charlottesville a dozen years before. Standing on opposite sides at the rear of the theatre, Cadiff and I ran toward each other and jumped into each other's arms. When we went backstage, the three actors were likewise celebrating jubilantly.

I quieted everyone long enough to tell them to be respectful when Dick and Max came backstage, as I knew they were going to. No rubbing Dick's nose in it.

I knew Dick was about to enter one of his crazed, red-faced phases that would come about whenever he had no idea what he should do. The next morning, he showed up with a band-aid on his ear, saying he had cut himself shaving. (Shaving his ear? We conjectured that, when he was shaving, Fran was telling him that he never should have dropped the show, and he turned to yell at her and the razor found his ear.)

Before I saw Dick that morning, Max had cornered me to let me know that *his* Fran had made him tell Dick of his involvement in the show and his intent to continue. This, of course, served to make Dick even more crazed. And then Freydberg delivered the *coup de grace* by approaching Dick as he was about to get in the car to go the airport and, without a word, showing him a phone message he had in his hand. It read simply "Bernie Jacobs."

Garlic to Dracula.

Freydberg and I were relieved we wouldn't be on their flight back to New York.

But we knew we'd be back there early the following week, and that, one way or another, the show would open off-Broadway later that season.

As for the Shuberts, they were indeed interested, but the first-refusal-of-Broadway-theatre clause in the event of a transfer that Dick had insisted on was a problem for them. We went to Dick and asked him to either get aboard or cut ties altogether; making a decision now was the only ethical thing for him to do. But he wouldn't budge. No more investment and no elimination of the troubling clause. He was in a position to play two ends against the middle and took full advantage of it.

Jujamcyn claimed it had, to date, put $30,000 into the show's development over a year and a half. We didn't have the time or leverage to dispute this inflated number, so we included it as part of the off-Broadway capitalization, which Freydberg and I set at $500,000. Jim cajoled Jacobs into agreeing that the Shuberts would invest a matching $30,000 regardless of Dick's refusal to drop his first dibs on a possible uptown move; had we been able to get rid of that provision, the amount would have been considerably more. We were hamstrung. Max, of course, came in with a healthy piece of what was needed, and Jim made a few "associate producer" deals, one with his longtime lyricist-director partner Richard Maltby, Jr. and another with a funding source of his from "Baby," and we started putting money in the bank.

Finding a suitable off-Broadway theatre was a bit of a challenge. When we returned from Chapel Hill, a scaled-down production of "Pacific Overtures" was about to open at the Promenade on the upper west side, which was the theatre and location we really wanted, and every indication was that William Finn's "In Trousers" would follow it there once the Sondheim revival closed. And, of course, "Little Shop" was still going strong at the Orpheum.

The most likely prospect was the Minetta Lane Theatre in the West Village, where the Circle Rep production of Lanford Wilson's "Balm in Gilead" had transferred the prior month and was playing to considerably less than full houses. Given its huge cast, and the unusually large payroll it carried with it for an off-Broadway show, its prospects for a long run appeared dim, and before long it posted a closing notice for early January. We had already negotiated a backup contract with the Minetta Lane's owners, so we were now set to go.

While New York is the destination that almost every show wants to reach, I do have to point out that it's much less fun to produce a show there than in places like Chapel Hill. Here's an example why. Our contract with the Minetta Lane stipulated that if the show exceeded a certain weekly gross, our rent would jump up. One Sunday night, just before the final performance of the accounting week, one of theatre's owners or management team called in to the box office treasurer, Hal Luftig, and asked what the weekly gross would be. When Luftig told him the number, he knew it was just under the amount needed to hike the week's rent. He told Hal to buy the necessary tickets for that performance in his name so as to push the gross over the magic number for the week. In an unheard-of move by a New York City box office treasurer, Luftig refused. I was standing in the box office at the time and heard the whole thing. I applaud Hal Luftig to this day for his integrity and am pleased that he has gone on to have a long career as a respected producer in New York theatre.

Another example: our set in North Carolina cost $5,000 and worked like a charm. To have the same set, with a few flourishes, re-built in New York, in a non-union shop no less, cost $35,000. And the central component – a simple wagon that moved straight down-stage and straight back – didn't work. It kept getting stuck, and the shop wanted additional monies to come and fix it. Every time. When it *still* didn't reliably work, we had to hire an independent technical supervisor to finally solve the problem. Ka-ching. There were days when Freydberg and I were more consumed with look-ing in every direction to keep the show from being ripped off than in being nurturers of the creative process and planning for opening night and beyond.

Creatively, there was very little to do after Chapel Hill other than for Cadiff to adapt the staging for the Minetta Lane, and the entire process went smoothly.

Less than three weeks after "Balm in Gilead" closed, we began previews and the actors started becoming acclimated to the differ-ent feel of playing the show in front of New York audiences and making adjustments as necessary.

Howard Ashman came to the second preview performance unannounced; somehow I didn't see him, but I did see the credit card receipt for his ticket (I, of course, would have comped him had I known he was coming). I never found out what Howard thought of the show, but I deduced he at least liked the score as a few days later Rupert received a call from him asking if he would be inter-ested in collaborating with him on a project. More married to Jerry Colker at that point than Howard apparently was to Alan Men-ken, Rupe declined, a decision he later probably regretted. Actually, knowing both of their personalities, I think it's at least possible they might have worked well together.

Bill Craver (by then a theatre lit agent, remember) also came to a preview one night and, afterwards, he and I went to a nearby restaurant for a bite to eat. Bill had very much liked the show and said that, if the opportunity ever arose, he'd love to represent the writers and director. I asked him if he wanted their phone numbers. He declined, saying he would never make an overture to steal another agent's clients. Those of you who have worked in the industry know how incredibly rare this type of integrity is, particularly among agents, but that's why I respected Craver so much. He did, of course, add that if they wanted to call him, he'd happily accept their calls. (They did, and he did.)

Our preview performances kept getting better and better as we approached critics' weekend, with opening night on Tuesday, February 5.

Frank Rich came to the Friday evening performance prior to the opening, and the show played better than it ever had. As far as I was concerned, one way or another, our fate was sealed that night. Whatever happened, we gave him the show we wanted to.

We didn't have a formal opening night party; instead, everyone headed to Charlie's to await the reviews. For the producers – Freydberg, myself, Weitzenhoffer, and Maltby – there was the obligatory stop at Ash-LeDonne, the ad agency handling the show. There, we were handed copies of the *Times* review. "It's mixed," they told us.

In short, Rich loved the first act but was disappointed by the second. Whereas the *Raleigh News & Observer* critic had felt that the betrayal of the three guys' true talent had come from within them, Rich felt the second act fell into the cliché of Hollywood corrupting the integrity of their talent. Musically, he compared the angry guy's metamorphosis song when he becomes a father unfavorably to "Soliloquy" from "Carousel" (maybe there *is* room for only one song expressing that emotion in the musical theatre canon, who knows). And, rather ironically considering my first impression of it back on the LIRR, he found the final number, "I Don't Believe in Heroes Anymore," "vastly overreaching." I knew it wasn't, that all the words necessary to justify it were in the script, but the content of the show was so dense that not even someone as perspicacious as Rich had picked up on it.

Although the following week he would name us a "Critic's Pick" in the *Times*, with additional positive things to say, he ended his review by equivocating and saying he looked forward to what the shows' creators would be up to next.

I immediately went into a funk, so much so that when we went to Charlie's and the other print reviews were circulating, it took me a while to realize that Clive Barnes in the *Post* and Douglas Watt in the *Daily News* had both written raves. (Watt was particularly surprising as we never dreamed he would like it; a rumor started circulating that his wife had hated it and wanted them to leave at intermission, but he had refused, so she left anyway and he wrote the rave as a way of spiting her. I guess anything's possible.)

This didn't get me out of my funk, though. A handful of us later walked over to Sardi's for one final drink, which, by that point, I certainly didn't need. On the way, I started trying to kick down the Shubert Theatre when we passed it. I didn't succeed.

After a few hours of restless sleep, I returned to Ash-LeDonne in the morning for the traditional producers' post-mortem where we determined how we'd proceed. The television reviews had been mostly negative and snarky, but some other positive print ones had come in overnight. We clearly had a mixed bag.

Maltby was the first one of us to offer a concrete opinion. Putting his hand to the side of his face in his trademark fashion, he confidently said, "I think we have a smash."

I looked at him and responded, "I think you're crazy." I had been in this position before, and I knew that, without a full endorsement from the *Times*, we had a challenging road ahead. I was still in my funk, but I wasn't wearing tinted glasses. Seeing that I was feeling pretty crappy about things, Jeff Ash, one of the three partners in the agency and the son of Broadway advertising legend Ingram Ash, asked to see me alone in his office.

"However you feel now, I just want to tell you that I'm aware, and you should be too, that this show never would have gotten on without your determination," he told me. I took it as the compliment it was meant to be, and I appreciate his words of acknowledgment to this day.

Back in the meeting, we knew we had enough positive ammo to try to make a go of it. Jeff Richards would work on getting interviews for the three actors (a terrific, lengthy feature would appear in the *Times* the following week) and Jim would put together a tv commercial with the limited funds we had to spend. (Part of Freydberg's and my arrangement was that he'd primarily handle the marketing of the show given his self-proclaimed expertise.)

Here's where the Catch-22 of producing a show off-Broadway comes in, unless the show is an out-and-out smash. Advertising budgets are limited out of practical necessity. Why? Because with only several hundred seats to sell rather than the 1,000 to 1,500 in most Broadway houses, the potential upside gross is also limited. There's no point in spending more promoting a show than what the ads can generate in ticket sales. *Plus, the costs for ad space and airtime for Broadway and off-Broadway are mostly the same.* Not to mention the costs of shooting a commercial.

Which is why Jim couldn't use the show's best selling point – its music – in the tv ad. Instead, he had Colker write a "comedy" bit for the three guys. And it was the worst writing Jerry had done for the show. As a result, the commercial that New York metro area tv audiences saw was maybe the first televised ad to ever *unsell* a show. On this, there was general agreement within the company; it hardly generated even a slight bump at the box office.

This meant word-of-mouth was crucial. The show definitely had its ardent fans, and for a while their word-of-mouth sustained it. But there were also those who were turned off by it. The most amusing of these was a man who had bought a ticket front and center, but 20 minutes in came to the realization that "3 Guys Naked" wasn't the type of naked entertainment he was seeking, so he stood up and shouted "This is bullshit!," then stormed out to the box office to demand a refund.

But, in retrospect, I realize what was turning off a large segment of the naysayers was that the show hit an unsettling nerve in them. I had been wrong in my initial fear about how it would play to audiences in North Carolina as opposed to Manhattan. My theory is that many of the audience members who could afford to pay $35 a ticket (which was a lot back then) for an off-Broadway show had *themselves* compromised their dreams and talents for the almighty dollar and maybe in some cases fleeting fame, just as the three guys did. The audiences in Chapel Hill may not have achieved their dreams (or even started on the road to them), but they hadn't sold out. We didn't lose them in the second act.

I'm convinced that, in New York, our show had the same hitting-too-close-to-home problem that many think had been inherent in the Prince/Sondheim musical, "Merrily We Roll Along," a little over three years earlier.

For all that, we were able to run for five months, finally closing at the end of June. Thanks to record producer John Yap, we were able to cut an original cast album, and "3 Guys" has gone on to have several other productions, of which I've seen two, one in Toronto and one in Los Angeles. (I wish I had seen the Donmar Warehouse production in London in 1989.) I had always dreaded the thought of what productions without Bakula and Kassir would be like, but the performances were nowhere nearly as painful as I had imagined they would be.

The show is very much grounded in 1980s culture and mentality, so it's rarely done any longer given how dated it has become. It was, though, given a production in a small theatre in London in 2015.

I have no idea how it played, but the Finborough Theatre description of it is the best I've ever read: "This funny, vulgar and quintessentially 1980s show traces through stand-up, sketch and song the rise of three young stand-up comedians chasing the American Dream in a world where there are no heroes left."

It's all too rare – and, hence, very gratifying – when writers and critics "get it," when they accurately understand the essence of your show exactly as you intended it. Of all that was written about our original production of "3 Guys," one sentence stands out in my memory. It was Kevin Kelly's final one in his Boston Globe review:

"I left the theatre humming the future."

The Third Definition of "Lawyer"

One of my most treasured relationships in the theatre industry was with Norman Rothstein, a longtime general manager on Broadway who had as sharp a brain for the business as I had ever encountered and a down-to-earth sensibility and presence that was refreshing.

Ironically, Dick Wolff had been a school classmate of Norman's growing up. You could hardly call them friends, though, but rather colleagues who tolerated each other. Norman called Dick "Richard." Dick habitually referred to Norman as "a pants presser." None of us at Jujamcyn could ever figure out what that meant, except we knew from his tone that it wasn't complimentary.

I remember one time Norman called me, mystified.

"Stephen, tell me what I'm missing here. I'm comparing theatre deals for 'Tap Dance Kid' [a 1983 musical he was managing] and Richard wants more for the Martin Beck than the Shuberts want for the Broadhurst. I mean, *please…*"

For those unfamiliar with Broadway geography, the Beck (since renamed the Al Hirschfeld) was in a less desirable (alone on the other side of 8th Avenue) location than the Broadhurst, which is in the middle of one of the two most exciting streets in the theatre district, surrounded by four other theatres and Sardi's. No wonder Norman was baffled.

Perhaps needless to say, "The Tap Dance Kid" opened at the Broadhurst, not the Beck. Regardless, one day Norman called me and told me about a new play he had been hired to manage. It had been written by a young woman from Alabama named Margaret

Beddow Hatch and its "producers" were a brother-and-sister duo from Texas with no theatrical experience. The "sister" had been the author's roommate in college and had fallen in love with the play, which was entitled "Stem of a Briar." (The play's title, curiously enough, is the third definition of "lawyer" in some older dictionaries.) Norman felt it was necessary to partner them with professionals and thought I'd be a good fit with the play. At the time, it was being given a professional production on the campus of highly regarded Kenyon College in rural Gambier, Ohio.

As it happened, Jujamcyn's literary manager, Barbara Laney, had heard of the production and had already scheduled a trip out to see it. I had come to trust Barbara's opinion of straight plays (not as much musicals, which are more conceptual), so I decided to wait for her report.

As it happened, she returned to New York quite enthusiastic about the play, which was unusual for her. I should have immediately gotten on a plane and flown to Ohio, but I didn't, which I'd later regret. Instead, I read it and was blown away by the young author's writing. It was distinctly southern, and her eloquent use of language was on a par with Tennessee Williams at his best.

Especially since Barbara and I were in agreement (which we weren't always), there was no problem getting Dick to give me the green light to proceed. I called Norman and told him we were interested in getting involved. I also sent a copy of the script to Ray Larsen, as I thought it would strongly appeal to his sensibilities. It did, and Ray hopped aboard.

As I had suspected from various comments Norman had made, he and I would have to be the ones to push the project forward. The "brother" of the Texas tandem, Tim, took a back seat, but the "sister," Sharon, jumped into every aspect of the process. The problem was that she was naïve and overly enthusiastic about the project, which sometimes created, well, peculiar situations. Imagine a Texas cheerleader being given the Broadway sandbox and the New York singles scene to have fun in, together with her college roommate, and you kind of get the picture.

"Stem of a Briar," though, was a far superior play than what one expects a dilettante to show up with in New York. It was a memory piece in the grand Southern tradition, a father-son play, with the son trying to follow in the footsteps of his extraordinarily gifted father in the practice of law, but without either the passion or talent to do so. In Ohio, it had been performed in three acts, but soon afterwards was wisely reduced to two, and it was the second act where everyone seemed to think a problem was, although no one could define it, much less solve it.

The director at Kenyon had been a competent New York journeyman who, by all accounts, had done a respectable job. Sharon wanted to retain him for New York; Barbara wasn't so sure. The father, Roderick Denner III, had been played in Gambier by the accomplished Broadway actor John McMartin; everyone who saw it agreed he had done a stunning job but might be lacking the necessary stature the part requires. And the lead role, the son, Roderick Denner IV, had been played by a young actor named Robert Joy; Sharon thought he was fine, but Barbara strongly felt he needed to be replaced. Of course, since I hadn't gotten on that damn plane to Ohio, I couldn't offer an opinion.

The upshot? We decided to do another tryout production. I sent the script to Ed Sherin, who responded positively to it and offered us a spring slot in his 1983-84 season at the Hartman Theatre in Stamford, where he was Artistic Director. We reached a consensus that we'd keep Peters and McMartin for this round and replace Joy.

So the re-casting of Young Roderick became the chief focus. We must have auditioned every actor in New York who could play "young 20s." Since the buzz on the street was that "Stem" was Broadway bound, the search for this plum role took on a bit of a mystique within the acting community. Of course, this was nurtured by Sharon, and after several of the auditions, she would go up to the actor, hug him, and whisper in his ear. Huh? We knew she spent many of her evenings at Café Central and other Upper West Side singles joints, but she wouldn't mix business with pleasure. Would she?

Regardless, yet again there was no consensus choice among author, director, and individual producers. And Peters didn't have the clout to sway any of us; in fact, he was the most malleable of the group, which wasn't a good sign. And since I hadn't seen Joy in the role in Gambier, I had no basis for comparison.

Finally, in our collective brilliance, we settled on an actor who couldn't even audition because he was working in Japan at the time. The others were taking a blind gamble; but at least I had worked in a different capacity with Dennis Boutsikaris several years before, so I knew how talented he was.

The two choices we all agreed on were casting Michael Learned, who had gained fame in the '70s playing Ma Walton on the long-running television series "The Waltons," and Donna Bullock, who got the enthusiastic approval of those who had seen her in the Kenyon production, as Young Roderick's mother and sister, respectively. They were both terrific in the roles, and the warmth people associated with Learned from her "Waltons" image proved to be genuine offstage as well in this lovely lady.

McMartin and Boutsikaris were much more distant when not in character. McMartin was a quiet, private person, and pretty much kept to himself; he and I exchanged maybe three sentences in the five weeks we worked together. Boutsikaris just seemed to have a proverbial bug up his ass the whole time. It was easy to get the feeling he was disenchanted with either the role or the play or both.

But onstage, both were excellent. McMartin, especially, was better than I had ever seen him; he nailed the character in a meticulous way one didn't fully suspect from simply reading the script. The problem that existed with his performance was the predicted one that wasn't his fault and that he could do nothing about. The part did require *stature*, and, for all his brilliance, McMartin didn't have that. He didn't seem larger than life, which was essential for the audience to buy into the belief that Young Roderick would make the decision to go against who he is in order to try to live up to his father's example. It was heartbreaking because McMartin was so perfect in every other way.

The Hartman production was respectable in all aspects. Yet it needed to be dynamic. And the second act was still giving some people problems, although no one could say why. Personally, I thought all the proper beats were hit and that with the right father-son chemistry created by the right actors and director, the play would click on all cylinders. But the second-act issue wouldn't go away.

Now it was my turn at bat, without interference. My first step was to try to think of a director who could both serve the material and attract a star to the role of Roderick, Sr. As this type of traditional play wasn't being written or produced much any longer, I wanted someone who had worked in this genre and could guide Margaret from a place of experience in the process of making revisions.

I landed on George Roy Hill. Among his several Broadway credits as a director were the Pulitzer Prize-winning "Look Homeward, Angel" in the late '50s and Tennessee Williams' "Period of Adjustment" in 1960, also helming the film of it that followed. More recently, two of his films starring Paul Newman and Robert Redford had become part of the popular culture – "Butch Cassidy and the Sundance Kid" and "The Sting," the latter winning him a Best Director Oscar.

Word in the business was that he had soured on Broadway after the failure of his last show, the musical "Henry, Sweet Henry," which had definitely deserved a better fate when it opened in 1967. I figured if he could be lured back, this might well be the play to do it.

I called him, introduced myself, and asked if he'd be willing to read a script if I sent it to him. His response was to ask a question that no director had ever asked me when I approached them.

"Why do you think I'd be the right director for this," he inquired.

I told him because of his story sense and his known history of working well in shaping this type of material.

Apparently, I answered correctly because he said he'd take a look if I sent it over to his Manhattan apartment. I wasn't too optimistic about the degree of his interest, though.

Then, about a week later, the Jujamcyn secretary tells me that George Roy Hill is on the line for me. (Oddly, it's the journeymen who take a long time to respond; the ones at the top almost always do so in short order.)

I pick up the phone and Hill's first words are "Mr. Wells, that's quite a play you have there. Could you arrange a meeting for me with the author?"

I can and I do. But not before running down the office corridor punching the air. I think we got him!

He and Margaret hit it off terrifically and agreed to work together on revisions. Each of them occasionally called me to say how well it was going. Margaret did relay one minor oddity. The first act ends with the line "I love you, too." George told her he had always hated using the word "love" and wondered if she'd be willing to change it to "I do you, too."

I do you, too?

Oh well, may this be our biggest battle to fight.

A few months after they started working together and I had been given a current draft, Hill called me one day with a request.

"I would like to put together a reading of the play so we can hear it from the mouths of actors. Do you think you could messenger a copy of the script over to Paul Newman's office at the address I'm about to give you?"

165

I told him that I was pretty busy at the moment, but that I might be able to get to it before the end of the week.

And if you believe that, you have a serious problem with gullibility. Newman had it by the end of the day. I only delayed long enough to run down the corridor and punch the air again.

Next thing I know, a reading at Actors Studio has been scheduled, with Paul Newman playing Roderick Sr., Eric Roberts playing Young Roderick, and Joanne Woodward in the wife/mother role.

I then received another call from Hill a few days before the reading. He told me Newman would not permit any members of the producing team other than Sharon and me to be in attendance at the reading (Sharon because of her relationship with Margaret and me because I was the creative producer on the project). His concern, given that Actors Studio was known as a "creative space," was that having "big money" producers there could jeopardize the future of the project and inhibit the actors and the discussion afterwards. Hill said he hoped this didn't create a problem for me.

It did. A big one.

I now had to tell Dick and Ray that they couldn't come to the reading, not to mention poor Norman who had shepherded the project from its infancy. Norman, though, immediately understood and accepted it. Dick, I knew, wouldn't, but I wasn't prepared for how ballistic he went. Norman and I jointly broke the news to him.

Dick railed like Lear against the storm, but not nearly as eloquently. "Who does Paul Newman think he is?!!" he bellowed indignantly.

"Um…Paul Newman," I suggested, only making him angrier.

"Well, you tell Paul Newman that I own the play and if I can't be there, I'm not letting the reading happen."

"Richard, I have a playwright who's wrapped herself around a toilet and has been throwing up out of fear you'd react this way," Norman countered.

"And Dick," I said, "you don't *own* the play. You partially own the option to produce it," I tried to reason with him. But reason only tended to make him more furious.

Between us, Norman and I finally wore him down and got him to agree not to stop the reading. But he remained boiling hot at how he was being treated.

When Dick finally disconnected from the line, I said to Norman, "Don't you think the part about Margaret being wrapped around a toilet was a bit much?"

"Stephen…*please*," Norman replied. "I was desperate."

I was going to let Ray know the following morning, but my phone rang first, and Ray didn't even wait for me to say hello.

"I…AM…PISSED!" was how he greeted me. Ray was usually very soft spoken, so it was obvious that this dictum had hit a nerve. I was able to calm him down much easier than Dick, as he was able to understand the old saw "Where does an 800-pound gorilla sit? Anywhere he wants." If Newman had wanted the reading held at 3 a.m., that's when it would have been held.

Of course, it was held in the afternoon, and Actors Studio was packed with its members, many of whom were well-known playwrights, actors, or directors. Ellen Burstyn introduced the event. Both Woodward and Roberts embraced their characters. Newman, though, held back. He read the role in a kind of laid-back fashion, as if he felt that this wasn't the time or place to make interpretational choices as an actor. It thus became hard for a dynamic to be created between Senior and Junior, although the beauty of Margaret's language came through regardless.

What also came through was the deep and genuine warmth between Newman and Woodward, not only as appropriate in the characters they played, but as real-life husband-and-wife, during the break at intermission and throughout the post-reading discussion. The affection they displayed for each other bordered on being, well, cute.

I had attended many of these post-production discussions while a drama major in college and as an adjunct college professor at the time. And this one was exactly the same. Well, not exactly. Instead of students and professors, the participants were some of the major players in American theatre and film, with a famous director and stars listening to the comments of their peers, and none other than the legendary Elia Kazan moderating. It was kind of a "pinch me" moment.

Criticisms were generally fairly minor, except for one. The damn second act came up again. And not even *this* illustrious congregation of minds could put its finger on the what, why, or where.

Kazan tried to help by saying he had always found that if there was a problem in a play's second act, the seeds of it could always be found in the first act.

In the case of "Stem," everyone felt the first act was air-tight and everything in it led to the second. Yet given the eminent source of this insight, it couldn't just be dismissed. But not even Kazan could define where the issue might be, and nor could the assembled braintrust. Again, whatever it was that was leaving some people unfulfilled dramatically remained an elusive enigma.

Hill decided that he and Margaret should go back to their work sessions, which they did. A few weeks later he reported to me that Woodward very much wanted to do the play and was trying to talk her hubby into it, but that Newman was resisting a return to Broadway. I had figured that this would be the case as it's both a huge reputational risk and time commitment, not to mention financial sacrifice, for a major film star to commit to a Broadway play, especially a new one.

As fate would have it, I ran into Newman on an American Airlines flight to Los Angeles several months later. I was in the seat directly in front of him and, at some point as he was returning from a visit to the lavatory, I stopped him and introduced myself as a producer of "Stem." We engaged in a pleasant, relaxed conversation with him saying how much he admired Margaret's writing and had always enjoyed working with Hill. But he felt he was wrong for the part.

"He needs to be a big man of towering stature. I'm far too small in size [he was 5'10"] to be believable."

Huh? Here was Paul Newman telling me that he – of all people – didn't have the stature of greatness to project.

I told him he absolutely did, but the truth was that doing eight performances a week was anything but appealing to him at this stage in his career, right?

He insisted it was his lack of physical stature.

I asked, "What if we could make it only six performances a week?," but he didn't answer.

It turned out we both happened to be staying in L.A. at the Hotel Bel-Air, which I discovered when we ran into each other as we were checking in. I began to fear he thought I was following him to do a hard-sell. But we didn't cross paths again and, besides, that's not my style.

Sometime later, Hill called me saying he had been going to a lot of new plays on Broadway and that he almost always left the theatre thinking "Stem" was a better play. He and Margaret were still trying to figure out the second act, but it's hard to fix a problem you can't define. Hill said he sometimes thought we should just forge ahead and do it. Yet he hesitated.

The saga took a sad turn at this point. Hill had a film commitment he had to honor, so there was a pause in his and Margaret's work. By the time he had finished, Margaret had developed a brain tumor. She was still working, but not at the same level as she had been. Jujamcyn's option had lapsed, and I was now off producing television.

In the fall of 1989, Cleveland Playhouse staged a production of "Stem," and Norman had heard from Margaret that she had made significant changes to the script. I was living in Los Angeles at the time, but on one of my frequent trips to New York, Norman and I couldn't resist flying out to Cleveland to see the revised version.

Halfway through the second act, Norman turned to me and whispered in my ear, "We've been had." The changes were hardly significant and the production was a notch below what we had mounted in Stamford. Given what we both knew to be the deterioration of Margaret's health, we couldn't be angry, despite being in Cleveland for no reason.

At the time, I had no idea I'd be working with Margaret again within six months on a cable television series I was consulting on. She was a staff writer with a "Producer" title but was much different than the Margaret I had known. Her talent had diminished along with her health. She'd keep to herself most of the time and had to take long periods of rest.

Following the first season of the series, she went home to Alabama, where she died several months later at all too young an age.

As for "Stem," one of my two tv partners, Chris Auer, had also worked with Margaret, first on the daytime soap "As the World Turns" years before and more recently on the cable series I had worked with both of them on. He, too, was a fan of the play. We decided to try to option the film rights from her estate, and Chris would adapt it into a screenplay. He called Margaret's father, who agreed to license the rights to us. We signed the agreement during my wedding reception on Long Island in December of 1992.

While not dealing with the second act "problem," if indeed there even was one, Chris' script was faithful to its source, and we started trying to find a studio or production company to umbrella it. But at the first sign of interest, bullshit began, with the entity being more concerned with how the billing would read than with how to develop it while being true to its aesthetic. The only intelligent input we received on the script was from (*please…*) Norman.

Chris and I were both comfortable in television, and that's where our relationships were. The L.A. film industry was an enigma to us, and we had trouble getting our sea legs. More significantly, my willingness to put up with the egos and trade-offs and crazies that are omnipresent in the industry had reached its breaking point. The whole L.A. mentality was driving me back to the east coast to preserve my sanity and values. And on top of this, after almost a decade of trying to find the commercial exposure and status for "Stem" that I felt it warranted, my passion had faded.

Chris had his constraints as well. He needed to look for a concrete way of supporting his wife and six kids, the oldest of whom was approaching college age. He simply didn't have time to pound the L.A. pavement on spec playing "Try to Dodge the Latest Idiot."

And so, we pretty much let the project drift away. I feel confident that Margaret up in Heaven forgives us.

Take the Money and Run

Word of Maury Yeston's next musical following his award-winning "Nine" in 1982 had reached me before I even assumed my Jujamcyn role. Dennis Green, who was in the BMI Musical Theatre Workshop with him, had raved about some of the songs from it, especially one sung by a father to his newborn son entitled "New Words." Likewise, Howard Rogut had somehow gotten to know Maury, had heard part of the score, and, when it became clear that I'd be joining Jujamcyn, had begun telling me we *must* get the rights and produce it. Howard didn't get excited by much (other than *anything* to do with Mary Martin), has always had a good ear, and had earned my trust.

I was thus aboard the mission to obtain the rights to "One Two Three Four Five." It was a musical lark through the first five books of the Bible as experienced by a group of regular people. The nominal lead, who went by the name Ari, held a secret that the audience was let in on halfway through the first act. Another of the characters was so old that she was born before names had been invented and thus didn't have one; I was looking forward to battling with Actors' Equity over why we hadn't put a character name in the actress' contract to specify whom she was playing.

Before long I was treated to Maury playing through the entire show for me. It was an amazing through-composed achievement, both musically and performance-wise with Maury singing all the roles and, at one juncture, keeping three counterpoint melody threads going at once. The score was infused with wit as well as emotion. In the coming months, I probably heard him perform it

20 or so times and I never tired of it. His one-man, one-piano performance was one of the best shows in town.

Maury's agent was Flora Roberts, so it was no surprise that the option agreement for Jujamcyn to acquire the first-class rights was a challenge to negotiate. To many people on many occasions, Florabelle (as Howard and I called her behind her back) seemed certifiably neurotic, yet her stable of A-list clients from Sondheim on down testified otherwise. I was uncomfortable when Dick decided to have lunch with her at the Russian Tea Room to resolve a few final deal points, but somehow both survived and so did our pending rights to the show. Soon, Jujamcyn cut a $15,000 initial option payment to Maury (via Florabelle, of course) and we were officially set to proceed.

Maury, Howard, and I wanted to start by doing a workshop of the material for the creative and developmental reasons workshops *should* be done. Dick went along for the all-too-common wrong reason: so potential partners and backers could see it. (I planned to fight that out with him when the time came.)

First, though, we needed a director. And it needed to be a director who could create a whimsical musical universe for the biblical times in which the show takes place, much as Mike Nichols had done in the Adam and Eve segment of "The Apple Tree" in 1966. Naturally, Nichols himself wasn't available for eons, so it didn't make sense for us to try to interest him.

Despite having had a recent hit with him on "Nine," Maury said Tommy Tune wasn't a possibility we should consider either, for reasons he never explained.

Hal Prince was anxious to hear the show when I mentioned it to him (this was in his pre-"Phantom" days). I set a meeting for us with him at his Rockefeller Center office, but on the morning it was to take place I got a call at home from his longtime assistant, Annette Meyers, saying they needed to postpone. Hal's mother had died. This, of course, was in the pre-cell phone era, so I had no way of reaching Maury, who was already in the car that the service had sent to pick him up at his suburban home. I rushed over to Sixth Avenue and waited in front of Hal's building until Maury's car pulled up. I told him the news and the car ferried him back to the country.

After a respectable period of time had passed, the meeting eventually took place. Hal was smiling all the way through Maury's presentation, a couple of times turning to me and exclaiming "It's a real musical comedy!" (So many shows call themselves "musical comedies" when there's no wit and only feeble comedy.) But Hal was readying an off-Broadway revue about baseball entitled "Diamonds" at the time, to be followed by "Grind" on Broadway and "Phantom" in London, and he concluded he wouldn't be able to fit this show into his schedule for the next two to three years.

But there was one A-list director who was both available and interested when we had Maury play the show for him in one of the William Morris Agency conference rooms. Gene Saks had handled musical comedy deftly in the past and had staged some of the late '60s and '70s biggest hits. He and his agent, the legendary Biff Liff, were all but giddy throughout the presentation and Gene immediately expressed interest in coming aboard.

Our deal with Saks was relatively simple to negotiate, largely based on his and other top directors' prior deals. But there was a catch, and it had nothing to do with us. It was often common for a director to share in the bookwriter's percentage if he was developing a new musical with the author. This arrangement had become standard on most all Hal Prince shows after he shifted his primary focus from producing to directing. Once he began doing what came to be known as "concept musicals," he was usually the conceptualizer as well as the director, so it made sense that he would get fifty percent of the bookwriter's percentage. (Traditionally, on a musical, each component of the creative team – bookwriter, composer, lyricist – receives 2% of the gross, for a total of 6% overall. But

I have long maintained that the formula should be revised into four equal parts: bookwriter, composer, lyricist, *and* conceptualizer/ structuralist. This strikes me as a much fairer split, especially since the bookwriter/structuralist doesn't share in any of the outside monies the composer and lyricist might earn from their songs even when the basic concept for a song comes from him. This function is entirely different than writing the dialogue within a scene and should be financially acknowledged in some way. But I digress…)

Biff thus wanted Gene to not only get his director's percentage, but a piece of Maury's as well. My view of it was that Maury was getting 6% of gross since he had created the show by himself, so if he were to give one of those six points to Saks, he'd have what is called a "kick yourself on the way to the bank" deal; it only matters if the show is a hit and, by having an A-list director who's right for the material, the chances of it being a hit are greatly increased.

But Maury was adamant that the concept and structure of the show were entirely his creation and there was no reason for him to give any of it away. For all his musical talent and sunny energy, he also packed a tremendous ego into his diminutive frame. Yet Biff was equally firm in his view on behalf of Saks. So another lunch meeting took place at the Russian Tea Room, this time between Florabelle and Biff. I don't know which one picked up the check, but neither left happy. Neither would budge, and Saks was out. This, of course, left Howard and me unhappy as well.

When I told Dick that Maury and Saks had reached an im-passe, he demanded I get Maury on the phone for him. I went to the phone by the sofa in his office and called. Maury's then-wife answered and I told her Dick would like to speak with Maury.

"I'm sorry," she said, "can you tell Dick he's in the bathtub right now with his rubber ducky and can't talk."

I turned to Dick and relayed the message.

"He's in the bathtub with his rubby ducky and can't talk right now, Dick."

Predictably, Dick's face reddened. "I don't care about his rubber ducky! Have him call me!"

This was one of those moments when I had to pinch myself to remember that I was really working in the top echelon of Broadway theatre.

When Dick calmed down, he realized he couldn't alter the outcome. Saks was out and our search for a director who could handle Broadway, whimsical material, and Maury was back on.

Maury had taken to calling me at home late at night on matters that dealt with the show and also ones that didn't, often wanting me to guess what great idea or wonderful news he had. One such call resulted in my learning, after several wrong guesses, that his wife had passed her driving test. Another one started with him telling me he had thought of the perfect director for us.

"Who, Maury?"

"Guess."

"Just tell me, Maury."

"I'll give you a hint. This person knows more about musicals than anyone else."

A few minutes later, after several wrong stabs at it, I told him I gave up.

"Barbara Streisand!" he exclaimed. "Isn't that brilliant?"

"Go to sleep, Maury."

Meanwhile, Florabelle was trying to sell Maury on another client of hers, Gerry Guiterrez. Guiterrez at the time was one of the hottest of the "new breed" directors, having established an ongoing relationship with Playwrights Horizons and its Artistic Director at the time, Andre Bishop. He had also caught the attention of New York critics, especially with his then-current hit, Wendy Wasserstein's "Isn't It Romantic?"

Maury met with him and was sold. I had my doubts, though, because, talented as Gutierrez was, his success to date had been based on straight plays, which are totally different animals from musicals. But I didn't have any better ideas and I knew we needed to get this project off the launching pad. Besides, we'd soon see his work in a low-risk workshop production, wouldn't we?

Well, no, it turned out we wouldn't. Because somehow Larry Gelbart had heard of the project and was interested in collaborating on the show with Maury. I wasn't sure it needed a librettist, but the chance to bring in a writer of Gelbart's stature was hard to turn down. Still, Maury wanted to see how his through-composed show, as conceived, would work before he determined if he wanted, or needed, to collaborate with Gelbart. Fine by me. Again, nothing really to lose.

Dick never understood why it wasn't *his* ultimate decision to make. The "muscle" here was Maury's, and while he wasn't opposed to bringing Gelbart in, he just wanted to begin the process working on a blank canvas by himself, with a director's support. I respected that. And, further, he had been told by us initially that he could. But I knew I couldn't win an argument with Dick over caving to an artist's ego given Dick's own insecurities.

The result, you guessed it, was a stalemate. Dick vs. Maury. Work on the project came to a halt for the remainder of the time Jujamcyn held the option. It was "3 Guys Naked" all over again, but without a Freydberg card to play.

At this point, it had been several months since I had left the employ of Jujamcyn and begun overseeing the projects I had in active development through an executive producer's contract that paid me $1,000 a month for the one straight play ("Stem") and $1,500 a month for each of the two musicals ("One Two Three Four Five" and "Hagar") still in the hopper and then percentages of gross and net if any were produced. Of course, my contract, as it pertained to "One Two Three Four Five," was held in suspension once active development ceased.

In 1987, I was semi-happily becoming more ensconced in the world of network television development when word reached me

177

that Dick was being replaced as president of Jujamcyn by Rocco Landesman, whom I had come to both know and respect in my Broadway travels. He and Michael David were the *de facto* heads of Dodger Theatricals (David is now formally its president), an energetic producing group that had its origins at the Brooklyn Academy of Music but was then making its presence felt on Broadway with "Pump Boys and Dinettes" (1982) and "Big River" (1985). I had become friendly with most of the group's principals, who were consummate theatre pros and among the nicest guys on the street.

One day, a few months into his Jujamcyn tenure, Rocco called and asked me to come over and meet with him about a project – and that project was "One Two Three Four Five." I had heard that Manhattan Theatre Club had become interested in it and that, behold and lo, Maury had actually decided to collaborate with Gelbart prior to a workshop. It seemed Jujamcyn now wanted to become involved again. Of course, I still had a valid contract to executive produce.

I arrived at Rocco's office and noticed that Jack Viertel, whom Rocco had smartly hired for my old position (but with much more latitude), was also to be part of this meeting. Rocco immediately assured me that he would honor my contract. But he added that he was also willing to buy me out if I preferred. I responded that I'd of course need to know how much he was offering before even considering it. He then pulled out two pieces of paper, handed one to me, and said let's each write a number we thought would be fair. Naturally, I didn't want to lowball the amount I proposed, but I also realized that right now this show, as with all shows at this early stage of development, was worth nothing on the open market…and it might never be. On the flip side, a smash hit would result in my percentage being well into six or even seven figures.

I wrote $25,000.

Rocco wrote his number, then said we should exchange what we had secretly written, which we did.

He had written $15,000.

Inwardly, I smiled, because that was the number I had in my mind all along. But I tried to keep a poker face. We just looked at each other.

"Want to split the difference?" I asked.

"No, I think I like my number," Rocco responded.

At this point, Viertel's curiosity prompted him to ask to at least see the two numbers we were talking about.

Rocco reiterated that, alternatively, he would still monetarily honor my contract even if it was Jack who would now oversee the show's development for Jujamcyn (as it should be) along with Lynne Meadow of Manhattan Theatre Club. The choice was mine.

I asked for a few days to think it over, and Rocco was fine with that. As I was leaving his office, though, I did ask one question.

"Is Gutierrez still directing the workshop?" I queried.

"Yes," said Rocco.

This pretty much sealed my decision to take the buyout. I had been able to have several conversations with Gerry after he came aboard a few years earlier and my initial hesitations had morphed into instinctual concerns. It was hard to point at one thing he said that gave me the sense that he was applying too much grounded straight play thinking to staging a musical that would have to float on whimsy, but I had lost confidence that he was the right director for the show.

Less than a week later, I called Rocco and told him I'd take the $15,000.

The Manhattan Theatre Club workshop indeed materialized in short order. Howard, who was still in the employ of Jujamcyn, primarily serving as the house manager of the St. James, observed its evolution in rehearsals and told me it wasn't going as we had hoped.

Naturally, I was anxious to see for myself, so I attended one of the public performances. Guiterrez had cast several of Broadway's A-list musical actors, but, as I had feared, the whole enterprise remained earthbound, which was deadly for this material. I saw Gerry afterwards and we exchanged pleasantries and a few laughs after I jumped backwards from being startled when his small dog popped out of his shoulder bag and started yapping at me.

Whatever insufficiencies Gerry had as a stager of musicals were insignificant in his distinguished career. In the next decade, he'd go on to stage two definitive productions of revivals for his old friend Andre Bishop at Lincoln Center and then on Broadway: "The Heiress" in 1995 and Albee's "A Delicate Balance" in 1996. I had seen Alan Schneider's original production of the latter starring Jessica Tandy and Hume Cronyn in 1966 and found it coldly stylized yet somewhat interesting; Gutierrez made it accessible and spellbinding.

Soon after "Balance," he tried his hand at another whimsical musical, a Broadway revival of "Once Upon a Mattress" starring Sarah Jessica Parker in the role Carol Burnett originated in 1959. *Times* critic Ben Brantley used adjectives such as "misbegotten," "feels weary," and "distressingly wan" in describing the production and noted that "Mr. Gutierrez seems to have no clearly defined point of view toward the material." All of these observations could accurately be applied to his staging of "One Two Three Four Five" as well.

But I don't think he was solely responsible for the workshop's problems. I never did find out what the specific dynamics of the Yeston-Gelbart collaboration were, yet it became apparent that it was anything but harmonious, and obviously Gutierrez didn't have a unifying vision that might bring them together. There was every reason why these two major talents should have made a great pairing (unlike that of Howard Ashman and Marvin Hamlisch a few years earlier, the incompatibility of which was predictable). I have no idea what Maury's thoughts about it were. And as to Gelbart's, all I know is what he told a friend as he was beating it back to L.A.

"I'd forgotten how dangerous short people can be," he quipped.

What the Hell Is He Doing?

Most of the embarrassing incidents that I experienced during my time in New York theatre had an element of humor attached to them. One that didn't was an audition of a new musical in an author's apartment on the Upper West Side in 1984.

Flora Roberts had asked me to fly to Chicago to see a musical she was representing that was in development at Northwestern University. It was about Al Capone and had a book by John Weidman, whose credits included "Pacific Overtures," with music and lyrics by Robert Waldman and Alfred Uhry, who had received a good bit of recognition for their 1975 musical, "The Robber Bridegroom," which had a successful year-long national tour and ran for four months on Broadway.

I told Florabelle I'd indeed fly out and see one of the performances at Northwestern. I didn't know it until I arrived, but she was there the night I was, too. So was Andre Bishop, who at the time was Artistic Director of Playwrights Horizons. Flora positioned Andre and me in seats on either side of her, attendants to the queen.

Although the show, called "America's Sweetheart" (not to be confused with the short-lived 1931 Rodgers & Hart musical of the same title), didn't work, I thought that it might if numerous revisions were made. I've always had a preference for shows where I could see brains at work, and that was the case here; without being heavy-handed, it was a serious musical.

When I got back to New York, I wrote a three-page, single-spaced memo to the authors giving my candid thoughts and detailing suggestions concerning both content and structure. I sent it to Flora to give to them and they told her to thank me for taking the time to do it.

Cut to several months later after revisions had presumably been made. Knowing the respect that both Barbara Laney, our literary manager, and I had for what the writers were trying to achieve, Florabelle called to say she would like her clients to play through the score for us in one of their apartments. Only this time she wanted Dick to be there, too.

So the three of us arrived at the designated apartment (I forget which of the authors' it was) and exchanged pleasantries with Weidman, Uhry, and Waldman, who then began the playing of the score, interspersed with brief narration.

About two numbers in, Dick interrupted and asked if he could use the restroom. So Barbara and I chatted with the three writers about the show while he was gone. He returned and the presentation continued.

After another two songs had been played on the piano and sung, Dick, seeming increasingly agitated, said, "Excuse me, I need to use the restroom again." Barbara and I looked at each other as if to say "What's going on?" We reverted to more chatter with the writers, which was a little more awkward this time.

Dick returned and another few numbers from the show were performed. Then he stood up once again and excused himself to go to the bathroom.

The situation had gotten so weird that I finally felt I needed to acknowledge the awkwardness of it to the confused writers who, despite their facades, had to be offended by now. Barbara and I both made clear that we had no idea what was going on.

This time, Dick re-emerged and said he was sorry but he had to leave because he had an important meeting that he didn't want to be late for, but told the authors that Barbara and I would stay and hear the rest. And, with that, he exited.

I wished I could evaporate right on the spot. There's no excuse for being rude to anybody, but especially not in this way to accomplished professionals. But this wasn't only rude, it was bizarre. Barbara and I did our best to apologize for his behavior and expressed our total befuddlement over what just happened.

We obviously weren't going to make Waldman, Uhry, and Weidman continue with the presentation as it now seemed pointless. All five of us were simply anxious to end this debacle of a meeting, which we did.

The next day, my phone rang and it was an enraged Flora. "Mr. Wells," she started, "I got a most disturbing report from my writers about what happened yesterday. Is what they're telling me accurate?"

I responded that unfortunately it was.

"I must reconsider ever doing business with Jujamcyn again," she said.

I was finally at a crossroads. At least I was thankful that the option to "One Two Three Four Five" had already been signed.

"I can't blame you for that, Flora. All I ask is that you realize that I had nothing to do with what happened and that you don't hold it against me personally going forward."

She acknowledged that she wouldn't.

"America's Sweetheart" was produced at the Hartford Stage Company the following year, but never made it to Broadway. Alfred Uhry went on to win the Pulitzer Prize for "Driving Miss Daisy" four years later and collaborated with Hal Prince and Jason Robert Brown on the much-lauded musical "Parade" in the late '90s. John Weidman collaborated on two more musicals with Stephen Sondheim and was co-creator of the award-winning musical, "Contact," also in the late '90s. Robert Waldman continued writing and orchestrating music for theatre and film. Following his presidency of Jujamcyn, Dick Wolff returned to working in the box office of the Shubert Theatre.

Time for a Change

During the summer of 1984, Peter Neufeld invited me to have lunch with him at Charlie's one day. Unbeknownst to me, he wanted to give me some sincere professional advice as a friend.

What he told me was that I had to leave Jujamcyn if I was ever going to be anything but frustrated. He had observed the road-blocks that Dick was putting up on promising projects and said that I deserved better. Deep down I had come to realize this myself, but I didn't want to admit the truth of it. I have always appreciated the fact that Peter cared enough to advise me as he did that day.

My exit from Jujamcyn was pretty much inevitable anyway. It wasn't until after the "3 Guys Naked" run in Chapel Hill (which I had used Jujamcyn vacation days for) that I approached Dick about an exit strategy. I first needed to lay some groundwork for a partial transition into the television world.

During the development of the "Hagar" musical, I had gotten to know Bruce Paisner, who was president of King Features Entertainment. One day Bruce let drop in passing that if I ever decided to get into television to give him a call. That time had come and I did. We met for lunch one day and worked out an arrangement that called for me to work part-time at King Features assisting in development of some of the parent Syndicate's numerous characters and properties for all media.

All I needed to make this work was to get Dick to agree to letting me continue overseeing the existing projects still in development on an independent contractor basis rather than as an employee. It was an easy sell, as it turned out. And, combined with my King Features deal, I would be increasing my overall income by about 35 percent.

As you've seen, each of the development projects would eventually fall off the table, but by the time that began to happen, I had been offered a full-time position with KFE developing network projects while still having the freedom to do theatre on the side, teach my adjunct course at Drew University one night a week every spring semester, and remain on the board of the WPA. It made not having an office and a position on Broadway much more palatable.

How Austin Pendleton's Penis Led to Frank Rich's Marriage

...And Other Tales of Yore

.

How Austin Pendleton's Penis
Led to Frank Rich's Marriage

I forget how I met her, but there was a young woman working for The Shubert Organization who was looking to move on from there. It was Gerry Schoenfeld who had "discovered" her at the Yale School of Drama and offered her a job. But she had war stories from working in the Shubert offices above their eponymous theatre, just as I did from my perch a few theatres away above the St. James.

We started meeting after work on the second floor of Sardi's to commiserate and unwind with a few of their strong drinks. I was amused by her sardonic take on things. She was frustrated and was considering advertising as an alternative career; in fact, she was interviewing with the ad agency repping Purina dog food and was tempted to take the job there if it was offered.

"It's the Shuberts or Puppy Chow, and Puppy Chow is winning," she said incredulously.

Her name was Alex Witchel and she ultimately decided against hawking dog food for a living. Although neither of us had a romantic interest in the other, we kept in touch after I left Jujamcyn and I invited her to be my date for the opening night of a new play at the Ritz the following spring.

The play itself was a rather forgettable trifle called "Doubles," set in the men's locker room of a suburban Connecticut tennis club where four middle-aged guys discuss marriage and sex while (continually, it seemed) getting dressed and undressed. The audience was thus treated to the quartet of excellent actors stripping to varying degrees: Ron Leibman, Tony Roberts, and John Cullum partially, and (God help us) Austin Pendleton fully and frontally.

Trying to work that sight out of our minds, Alex and I went to the opening night party, which had the usual superficial frivolity of an obligatory event that pretends not to be a wake until the reviews come out and confirm that's exactly what it is. We didn't wait for the critics' opinions to land with a thud and instead left early and walked crosstown. We *were* curious as to what Frank Rich's review in the *Times* would say, so we headed to a newsstand I frequented on the corner of 50th Street and Second Avenue where we ran into…Frank Rich.

I had met Frank in my third year of college through a journalist colleague, but in the years since we had become passing acquaintances rather than friends, which I thought was proper given our respective roles in New York theatre. We lived near each other on the east side and I would sometimes run into him at this newsstand.

We greeted each other and I introduced Alex to him. The *Times* was late arriving that night, so we stood there chatting for quite a while. Frank was anxious to see if his review of "Doubles" had been run without a copy editor deleting the word "penis" from his text. If it hadn't been for his curiosity about that, he would have already been continuing on his way home.

Frank had been dubbed by theatre insiders as "the butcher of Broadway," but, knowing him a bit and respecting his writing a lot, I always felt he was honest in his opinions, whether I agreed with him in a specific instance or not. And that is all you can ask of a critic. Yes, he had unparalleled power and could often kill a show with his words, but that comes with the job of being the *Times'* chief drama critic, whoever it is. The fault isn't the critic's, it's the theatre industry's. What other multi-million dollar business allows some of its products' fates to be determined by one person's opinion?

Anyway, the paper was finally delivered and the three of us stood there reading his review. The word "penis" had indeed made it through to publication and, though having written a dismissive review, Frank hadn't crafted it with any scathing denunciations.

"You were a lot kinder than I would have been," I told him.

He responded that it was too slight and innocuous a play for him to work up much ire.

The three of us had been together about 20 minutes when we parted, and I didn't think much about it after that. Until…

…Until I discovered several years later that Frank and Alex were married.

Apparently, a few years after that happenchance meeting, Alex had called him out of the blue and he remembered her from the night of the penis vigil. He was no longer married to his first wife then, so they started dating and then made it official in 1991.

The next time I came into contact with them was in the spring of 1999 after I had moved back east from my decade of financial rehabilitation and social servitude in Los Angeles. In May of that year, I was doing my annual duty as a Tony Awards voter and seeing as many eligible Broadway shows as possible prior to casting a ballot. The house lights had just come on after a performance of Martin McDonagh's "The Lonesome West" when I saw Frank and Alex, each wearing a goofy grin, approaching me from the other side of the front orchestra. We reminisced about that night in 1985 and I was pleased to see how happy they were in their marriage.

The three of us stay in touch at least once a year, and, from all indications, their marriage remains as strong as ever.

Come to think of it, though, I've neglected to find out if they ever thanked Austin Pendleton for his, er, part in this love story.

Dancing with the Bumsteads

While most of my work at King Features Entertainment was in network television development, much of it also involved interacting with the cartoonists whose work was the financial backbone of the parent King Features Syndicate, which was an arm of the Hearst Corporation. Several of them had comic strips that were already part of a deal with CBS to be adapted into prime-time animated specials, which I was to produce.

But their number one client had a passion to see his famous comic strip become a musical, and, although the Hearst Corporation management didn't take such a venture seriously, I became the logical person they asked to keep him happy, which they deemed to be vital since his contract was coming up for renewal.

In the 1980s, *Blondie* was still the most widely circulated comic strip in the world, a half century after Chic Young created it. Upon his death in 1973, his son, Dean, took over and has been writing it ever since.

When I entered the picture, Dean had already had several false starts at adapting it into a musical. He and I hit it off right away and quickly became good friends. He was open to trying new approaches and understood (unlike many of his peers) that a comic strip is static whereas a musical has to have an arc.

I loved that I could be utterly candid with Dean and that he wouldn't be offended. One time, in discussing Blondie herself, I told him, "You know, I think your father forgot to give her a real character" and his response was "Steve-o, I think you're right!," which he punctuated with a laugh.

This was one of the challenges in adapting the famous strip into a musical: Dagwood was the principal character whose humorous exploits would make for a star turn, yet Blondie was the title character.

Dean would make regular trips to New York from his Florida home and check into a suite at the Waldorf-Astoria. He'd call me and say, "Steve-o, how about lunch at the Bull & the Bear?" The Bull & Bear was a restaurant in the hotel where Dean was well-known, and the maître d' would constantly come over to our table with a bottle of wine and say "This is my friend" while patting Dean's shoulder and sloshing wine all over the table as he poured it. I'd say more wine ended up on the table by the end of our lunches than in our stomachs except that the lightheadedness I felt by then suggested otherwise.

After a few of these lunches, I said to Dean, "I can't drink too much today; I have work to do back at the office."

Dean shot back: "Steve-o, as long as you're working for the Hearst Corporation, when you're drinking with me, you *are* working.

Hearst management liked to joke that I was sacrificing my liver for the company. (Funny, guys.)

In the sober world, my close friend (at the time) and "3 Guys Naked…" director Andy Cadiff was going through a tough time financially and kept asking me if I had anything for him to do to make a little money. I offered him a role in the "Blondie" development and was candid in telling him the company's purpose was to humor Dean and that it probably wouldn't result in a directing gig.

Somehow, I finessed the question I inevitably got from management: Isn't this what we hired *you* to do? Cadiff came aboard at $1,000 a month and he and Dean hit it off immediately.

Cadiff had recently co-authored and directed an off-Broadway musical for Roundabout Theatre Company entitled "Brownstone" that had (undeservedly, I felt) received an unfavorable response from the critics. Much like my experience a decade earlier with "Dreamstuff," the commercial rights had already been gobbled up (by major theatre financier Roger Berlind), but the reviews signaled that it would die a premature death at Roundabout.

Its score was by Peter Larson and Josh Rubins (both of whom Cadiff had met at Harvard), Peter doing more of the music and Josh most of the lyrics, and it was exquisite. One of the saddest images I recall from my time in theatre was when I saw Peter on opening night after the reviews had come out and he was trying unsuccessfully to hold back tears. He was one of the most promising – yet already accomplished – young (if 42 is young) composers I ever encountered. But, with a wife and a young daughter to support, it was understandable that he couldn't afford to continue pursuing his passion in New York musical theatre. Within a few months, he had relocated to Springfield, Missouri and had taken a job as a news producer for a local television station. The theatre's loss.

Cadiff suggested that he ask Josh Rubins to write the lyrics for the "Blondie" musical, and I instantly said yes, although I didn't yet have any idea how I could pay him even a small advance. Despite having a Harvard law degree, Rubins was hoping to make his living as a theatre lyricist.

Dean was so happy with the elements that were coming together that he added a demand to his overall contract renewal terms: that Hearst provide a $100,000 development fund for the musical, over which I would have sole signature authority. They had no choice but to reluctantly agree.

In theory, I may have had discretion over how funds were spent, but Dean of course had the ultimate authority for it to be used however he pleased. So cue up the corporate junkets. Cadiff, Rubins, and I would fly to Florida at Dean's whim to spend a few days on his yacht, the *Cartoon*, or spend time at his yacht club in Key Largo, or drive up to his condo in Vermont. In between golf and tennis, we would actually squeeze in a little work on the show, providing Dean with more book ideas to take back to his studio and flesh out. While Dean wasn't a professional bookwriter, he understood the dynamics of a musical and, more importantly, was totally open to collaboration.

When we discussed possible composers, I came up with the suggestion of Galt MacDermot and it was met with unanimous agreement. I called Galt, arranged a meeting, and he signed on. I then arranged for the paperwork to be done by the Hearst attorneys.

Galt never went on any of the junkets with us, but, working with Josh, he turned out a score that, to my mind, was his best since "Hair," with an opening number that was second only in his canon to "Aquarius"; entitled "Morning Glory," it energetically and tunefully captured the long-established essence of the morning routine in the Bumstead household. He and Josh also managed to craft two strong solos for Blondie, which gave her star material without violating the limited dimensionality of the character. The most important thing they achieved, though, both musically and lyrically, was to give a contemporary feel to a comic strip that was more than half a century old at the time.

Through my loyal casting director, Leonard Finger, I arranged for Dean to have lunch with Bill Irwin about the possibility of him playing Dagwood when we reached that point. And Cadiff and I took Bernadette Peters' agent, Bruce Savan, to lunch at the Russian Tea Room to alert him to the project.

Still, Hearst had no interest in it. Yet again I was working for an entertainment company that was loathe to take risks. My perception of the project had evolved from its early days to now seeing potential in it, but the powers-that-be at the Syndicate and on the Hearst board were content with just having the rights to the hugely profit-generating comic strip locked up for the next eight or so years.

Soon, Cadiff was off to California to direct the initial production of the next Colker-Rupert musical at the Pasadena Playhouse, the commercial rights to which I had optioned with two partners (more on that in a coming chapter). Josh Rubins, needing to make a living, started putting his Harvard law degree to profitable use. And I found myself flying to Los Angeles almost every 10 days either on television business or to check in on the Colker-Rupert-Cadiff musical development. As a result, "Blondie" sadly got pushed aside, never to be returned to.

A Second Non-Profit

Sometimes you do a show and it fails, but years later the mere fact that it happened leads to other more positive ventures. Such was the case with my first show, "Wings," without which Buzz McLaughlin and I would probably have drifted apart after I left Charlottesville rather than become close friends and colleagues.

McLaughlin left Virginia in the late 1970s and became a professor of drama at Drew University, a small liberal arts college in Madison, New Jersey, a commuter suburb of New York City. In 1983, he asked me to come out from the city one night a week in the spring semester to teach a course in musical theatre writing, which evolved into a perennial gig. It didn't pay much – barely enough to cover my rental car – but the weekly interaction with college students energized me; it was a refreshing change from the day-to-day business of commercial theatre.

A few years later, McLaughlin had an ambitious idea to start a non-profit theatre in northern New Jersey devoted to the singular mission of working with playwrights and developing new plays. The Madison Board of Education had years before taken a former elementary school building offline and it sat half-empty (the other half housed a Montessori pre-school) on a parcel of land almost abutting Drew. The old gymnasium inside could be adapted into an ideal theatre space.

McLaughlin approached the school district's superintendent at the time, Lawrence Feinsod, with a proposal. If the school district let his new non-profit use the empty portion of the building rent-free, he would create a playwriting-in-the-schools program for the district without charging a fee. It could be a win-win. Feinsod, being something of a visionary himself, saw the potential in this relationship and gave McLaughlin his blessing and a handshake, which was as formal as their "deal" ever got. Suddenly, Playwrights Theatre of New Jersey, as it would be called, had a home.

McLaughlin asked me if I would be willing to join the theatre's board of directors as its president. The rest of the board would be comprised of local individuals with no experience in the theatre business. Some came from wealth, others came from positions of note in the community, including the mayor. Buzz felt the need for someone with a theatre background and experience in the not-for-profit sector to serve as a leader. I was excited by the concept he had for the theatre and readily agreed.

For the first few years of its existence, I served on the boards of two non-profits: the WPA and PTNJ. But the excitement of the new venture was making me re-evaluate what had become my minimal commitment to WPA. Kyle by now was much more confident of his leadership abilities and even wanted to produce the transfer of WPA's latest hit himself (we, as a board, felt safe in letting him since Papp had been doing it at the Public Theatre for ages and there had been no legal challenges).

The play was "Steel Magnolias," and, while I was uncertain of its commercial off-Broadway prospects, mainly due to what I thought was an overly maudlin second act, I sensed it would be endlessly produced in stock and amateur theatres everywhere. At my final WPA board meeting, I conditioned my vote of agreement on Kyle having a large enough capitalization so that if not even one seat was sold in the six performance weeks it would take for the WPA's full participation in subsidiary rights to vest, it could meet that benchmark. Of course, that never turned out to be an issue.

Back at PTNJ, it wasn't long before the town's mayor and I butted heads. The conservative view he expressed was that no commitment of money for *anything* should be made until the funds to cover it were securely in the bank.

"Then you might as well close the theatre before it opens, Ralph," I shot back, somewhat to his shock. Operating a theatre often means proceeding on faith; no theatre can function under a cash-on-the-barrelhead policy. You can't bring a show in production to a screeching halt if there's suddenly a shortage of funds on hand. Getting people outside the entertainment world to understand this, though, often isn't easy. I was being perceived by Ralph and a few others as one of those reckless, irresponsible show business liberals. Fortunately, I had Buzz backing me up and most members of the board believing in him and trusting his judgment, so the never-take-a-risk faction didn't get its way.

PTNJ opened and soon began finding its audience for readings, workshop productions, and, my personal favorite, its annual Young Playwrights Festival. Kids at all grade levels in the Madison public schools would opt into after-school, age-specific classes and would write a short play under the tutelage of a teacher provided by PTNJ. In the spring, two of the plays at each age level would be chosen to be performed by professional actors over the course of a weekend, preceded by a day of rehearsal with a professional director doing the staging and each fledgling playwright taking part in the process.

Some of these short plays would be light and simplistic, of course, while others dealt with more serious topics. One high school student memorably wrote about having had thoughts of suicide, providing an unexpected jolt of intense drama for the audience and a catharsis of sorts for her. The whole enterprise was a terrific educational experience for all involved and soon PTNJ began being commissioned by other New Jersey school districts to bring its afterschool playwrighting program to their towns. Before long, PTNJ had a director of education to coordinate it all.

McLaughlin also brought aboard a sharp young graduate of Northwestern who was drama director at a private elementary and junior high school in a neighboring New Jersey suburb. John Pietrowski fit in perfectly with the youth aspect of PTNJ, but he was also a professional actor and director who had administrative abilities as well. He would handle the day-to-day management of the theatre.

In the beginning, McLaughlin coordinated almost all of the new play selection, readings, and workshop productions himself. He was able to attract both new and established playwrights to PTNJ, with each script starting with a reading and then sometimes progressing to a "workshop," which essentially was a staged reading that involved one day of rehearsal and two nights of open "performances." After each, McLaughlin and the author would hold a discussion session with the audience; if the playwright lived in a distant part of the country, PTNJ would fly him or her in for the three days. Then, when a script's potential warranted it, full productions would be mounted, usually running three weekends each.

Several notable actors who lived in the area were attracted to PTNJ, including Peter Dinklage and David Strathairn. At one reading, audience members looked at their programs and saw the name "Julie Harris," and were then startled when they soon saw that it was *the* Julie Harris. What I most admired about this was that her appearance hadn't been promoted so as not to attract people who would come for the wrong reason. This was, after all, a theatre about writers.

Bill C. Davis, whose "Mass Appeal" had been a modest Broadway hit in 1981, came out to PTNJ for a reading of one of his subsequent plays, although he refused to participate in the audience colloquy afterwards. Most writers, though, weren't known entities and were chosen based solely on the potential of their scripts. And the great thing was that McLaughlin and his staff treated sprouting writers like Ben Ross with every bit as much respect as Bill C. Davis.

If you're wondering who the hell Ben Ross is, well, I can't say where he is now, but he wrote two plays back in elementary school that were chosen to be performed in the first two Madison Young Playwrights Festivals back in the mid-'80s. A photo of this little tyke deep in concentration, with furrowed brow and pen in hand, became my lasting image of the magic inherent in this program.

I'm convinced that when it expanded to other towns and counties, whose schools were willing to pay decent money for PTNJ's teachers to come to their communities, this program, more than anything else, is what eventually led New Jersey officials to designate PTNJ one of the state's "Major Arts Institutions," of which there were only four others: PaperMill Playhouse, Shakespeare Theatre of New Jersey (also in Madison), McCarter Theatre Center, and George Street Playhouse.

I finally resigned from the board in the very early '90s, as I was living in Los Angeles then and the commute to meetings became impractical. Soon thereafter, Buzz, contemplating a move to New Hampshire, stepped down from his position and was succeeded by Pietrowski.

When I moved back east and settled in New Jersey in 1998, PTNJ was continuing to flourish and had a revamped board, with the CEO of Atlantic Mutual Insurance Companies – a warm and knowledgeable arts aficionado named Kermit Smith – as its president. I was asked to rejoin the board and I did.

By now, the board had become more of a substantial oversight entity and I enjoyed simply being a member of it instead of its leader. My role became largely defined by being the buffer between PTNJ and its landlord, the Madison Board of Education, as well as the only member with a background in professional theatre. This came in particularly useful on the few occasions when Pietrowski became interested in developing musical properties, one of which had terrific commercial potential but was undermined by (yet again) a Yale School of Drama grad who, in his dual role as writer and director, was resistant to making changes. By now, I was all too familiar with the traits of most Ivy League creative types I encountered: tons of talent but too much of it unharnessed and undisciplined, and my energy to deal with it had faded.

Although constantly in precarious financial condition – a fate hardly uncommon among nonprofit theatres – PTNJ kept humming along despite repeated threats by the Board of Ed to sell the property it was housed on. In fact, as highly recognized as PTNJ was, I always felt it was underappreciated in Madison, as was Pietrowski. There were always residents who would show up at Board of Ed meetings complaining, usually about the school district "giving the space away" rather than selling it, thus placing no value on the educational programs that it got for free while neighboring school districts were eager to pay for the exact same programs for their students. The complaints came in many forms. For instance, when an edgy play by the respected playwright Lee Blessing was being presented, one old geezer came to a Board of Ed meeting and said that school facilities were being used to present "porn." Of course, it wasn't porn any more than "Cabaret" or "Equus" is porn, but it was up to me to defend it at the meeting, which I could easily do in good conscience. I tried to conclude my comments with a zinger at the old man's expense.

"But what I don't get, Gene, is that if you thought it was porn when you saw it, why'd you come back a second time?"

Inevitably, the day came when the Board of Ed did sell the building as well as the three athletic fields the property included. The buyer was a developer who built an apartment complex on the large vacant lot. The days of people coming to see theatre and the almost daily sight of kids playing on the fields while trains chugged by on the railroad tracks across the street were gone.

Another slice of small-town Americana had bitten the dust.

Doing a Show for All the Wrong Reasons

"There must have been a moment, at the beginning, when we could have said – no. But somehow we missed it."
–Guildenstern, in Tom Stoppard's "Rosencrantz and Guildenstern Are Dead"

It was on a drive to the Raleigh-Durham airport during the glorious days of the "3 Guys Naked" North Carolina tryout production that Jerry Colker and Michael Rupert finally told me the title of their next project, after having teased me about it for a couple of months. We all knew we wanted to work together again, even though our present show was still one step away from New York, and this was their way of feeding me tidbits and jerking my chain.

"It's called 'Mail,'" Colker said.

My immediate reaction wasn't at all what I expected. My heart sank. If I had to define why, I'd lean toward saying that the word had a yesterday feel to it for these tomorrow writers. Still, all I was reacting to was the title.

Eventually they played me the entire show, which was through-composed, and my takeaway was that it was a monumental achievement on Rupert's part. Almost every individual number delivered the goods – catchy, melodic, energetic. So why didn't I feel the passion for it that had overcome me when I first listened to "3 Guys Naked"?

I wasn't able to define it at the time, but I think it had to do with its premise. Of the three characters in "3 Guys Naked," the least ingratiating was the angry-guy comic, who had many of the personality traits of Colker himself (so casting him in the role when Tony Crivello bailed made for a natural fit). And, as nice a guy as he was, Colker could be a royal pain in the ass. So, if one-third of their first musical was based on Jerry, then, perhaps misguidedly, *all* of their second one was.

The show's premise was a writer, Alex, nearing thirty, disappearing for several months in order to "find himself" and not telling anyone of his whereabouts or communicating in any way. Upon Alex's return to his apartment, he finds stacks of mail that have accumulated in his absence. The most persistent letter-writers are Alex's girlfriend, his best friend, his father, and his agent, who sing of their life concerns as they relate to him and his absence.

I had hesitations, but I ignored them because I was desperate to re-create the "3 Guys" work experience and I strongly believed in the collective talents of Michael, Jerry, and director Andy Cadiff, and didn't want to abandon them. The fact that the show was of Broadway scale also appealed to me.

Susan Dietz was running the Pasadena Playhouse at the time, and, truth be told, she had the passion for the show that I didn't. She offered to mount it there in the spring of 1987, so a built-in, risk-free tryout added to the allure. Although I had no overwhelming desire to work with Jim Freydberg again, we all felt we owed it to him and to Max Weitzenhoffer to audition the show for them in case they were interested in coming aboard. By then, though, Jim had snuggled up to Max and his money and had created F.W.M. Productions with Richard Maltby as the third partner, and they were already involved in producing several shows. As I suspected, they weren't interested in "Mail," and thus I was free to approach a new partner.

I had known Michael Frazier for several years and respected him as one of the dying breed of gentleman producers. I arranged for the guys to audition the material for him, and he was sold.

The problem for me was that I was in New York and, at this point, I had a full-time job with King Features Entertainment, producing prime-time animation for CBS and developing character-driven sitcoms to try to move the parent Hearst Corporation into that market. Although my position required frequent travel to Los Angeles, I was still mostly distanced from the action, as was Frazier.

The show was primarily cast out of L.A., with Dietz and Cadiff leading the effort. And they put together a stellar ensemble, including Brian Mitchell (before he put Stokes in the middle) as the best friend and Robert Mandan (who had played Chester on the hit sitcom "Soap") as the father.

Mandan, actually, was the second choice for that role. The first was veteran character actor Barney Martin, who exuded vulnerability better than anyone. Early on, Dietz had arranged for a reading of the material in Beverly Hills, at the Canon Theatre, which she also ran at the time. The show was still in its formative stages, but its penultimate number, "Twenty-Nine Years Ago," in which Alex's father reveals the depth of his pain at the disappearance of his son given what had been happening in his own life during those months, was already in final form. Rupert had to stand in the front row, only a few feet from Martin on the stage, to guide him through the number. Martin's rendition, and the added human dynamic created by Rupert's gentle coaxing, resulted in one of the most moving experiences I've ever had in theatre. Talk about transcendent.

Sadly, we feared that, at this late point in Martin's career, he would be unable to reliably remember his lines for as long a time period as theatre necessitates. He could still do television – and did, including what was probably his most remembered role, as Jerry's father on "Seinfeld," from 1991 to 1998 – but in terms of theatre, we thought casting him in a sizeable role would be too risky. As for "Mail," Mandan gave a perfectly competent performance, yet he never came close to capturing the emotional depth Martin had conveyed in what was essentially the show's eleven o'clock number.

For Alex's girlfriend, the choice was a young singer who was deservedly on the rise named Mara Getz; with spiked hair and a "woman of today" feel, she broke the mold of the traditional ingenue. The role of Alex's agent went to Antonia Ellis, who in real life was Mrs. Jerry Colker; again, competent.

And along the way it was decided that Rupert himself would play Alex, a choice that seemed to make perfect sense given Michael's consistent success as a Broadway actor all the way back to 1968. At least he didn't have to learn the score and he never missed a beat. He was also terrific. In fact, it was an amazing *tour de force*: he composed nearly two hours of music and played the lead role that kept him onstage for almost the entire show.

"Mail" opened in Pasadena in the spring of 1987 and was an instant hit. Audiences went wild and sellouts were common in the nearly 700-seat theatre. For the most part, critics joined the party, too. Still…

While there were parts of the show that I never tired of seeing and I loved the score, the overall theatre experience was still lacking something for me. I had trouble understanding the over-the-top audience reaction to it. I had serious doubts it would be the same in New York. But both Dietz and Frazier were gung-ho.

In those days, between television projects and "Mail," I was essentially commuting back and forth between New York and L.A. on an almost-weekly basis, so I became a frequent presence in the production hub as we tried to determine the next step on the road to Broadway. When we closed in Pasadena in mid-summer, though, the path forward hadn't as yet defined itself clearly.

Dietz, who had had massive influence in the Los Angeles theatre community for the prior decade, was able to figure out how to bring "Mail" back for a return engagement in the late fall. When it re-opened, scalpers were able to command $200 per ticket. I was flabbergasted. But it was then that longtime Broadway producer and Kennedy Center chairman Roger Stevens saw the show and wanted it for the Center as part of the current subscription season at the Eisenhower Theatre, with a $1 million commitment to the show's New York capitalization. This was the big hitter we needed, and, while I still questioned whether the show was really as good as L.A. told us it was, I opened my mind to the possibility that I could be wrong.

The five-week Washington run was to begin in February. That meant we had to make a super-quick cross-country transfer. Unfortunately for me, the next two months were perhaps the busiest months I ever had working in television development, so my focus was, by necessity, split. Frazier and I would speak daily, though, and I kept stressing the need for him to make sure the deal with the Kennedy Center was a licensing of the rights, not a co-production of the Broadway limited partnership we had created but not yet fully funded. The difference was significant; we had no financial exposure in a licensing agreement whereas, even with Stevens' million-dollar commitment, we were still short on the Broadway capitalization but would be accepting personal liability as general partners and accepting the legal liability for losses without yet having access to the investors' funds.

I had thought Frazier was as adamant as I was about us not being left exposed, and maybe he was, but apparently Stevens didn't care. Or didn't focus on it. Dealing with Roger at this late stage of his career had its challenges as he was either entering senility or faking it so he could use it as a tool to influence business deals. I never did figure out which it was, but somehow the contract with Kennedy Center ended up being an out-and-out joint venture agreement. When we opened in Washington, the limited partnership still hadn't been closed since it wasn't fully capitalized. At this point we were flying without a net, even more so after a nasty pan from David Richards in *The Washington Post* that signaled we probably had a rocky road ahead of us on the east coast.

The formal partnership needed to be closed quickly before investors began asking that their money be returned, which was their right prior to its formation. This meant that we, the general partners, were on the line for the remaining capitalization.

Of course, I didn't *have* to sign it, but, even though I knew it would probably end up costing me money I didn't have, I felt I had come too far with the project to just walk away. I wanted a Broadway opening more than I wanted to make the smart financial choice for myself. But even a greater influence on my decision to continue was that I felt I was morally, even if not legally, obligated to Frazier and Dietz to not leave them holding the bag. This was something that, ethical as he was, my lawyer, Jerry Nussbaum, couldn't comprehend. I suspected the show was likely doomed, and I knew it would take me years to climb out of debt, but in the end it wasn't really a choice for me.

At least the subscription base at the Eisenhower insulated us from losses for the five-week Kennedy Center engagement. Traditionally, that would have been enough time to try to "fix" the show. But as the musical theatre form had evolved into a more conceptual entity in the 1970s and 1980s, it was no longer as "easy" as cutting a song, re-writing a book scene, replacing a dance number, and making other changes to sections of the show that weren't working. As Andy Cadiff astutely noted at one point, it's often a case of either "buying in" or not, of getting on the roller coaster and enjoying the ride, or of not liking the notion of it and hating each turn and dip it takes more than the last.

"West Side Story" had been a forerunner of this style of musical and the creative genius (among several) behind it was director-choreographer Jerome Robbins. As it happened, "Mail"'s gifted choreographer and member of the original cast of "West Side Story," Grover Dale, was currently developing (and would be co-directing) Robbins' Broadway retrospective with him for the following season. Grover, whose work on "Mail" was truly inspired and (I thought) unassailable, suggested he invite Robbins to a performance to get his advice.

Of course, we leapt at the chance. A quarter-century earlier, Robbins had come to the Washington tryout of "A Funny Thing Happened on the Way to the Forum," which was bombing there at the time, and had famously told Prince and Sondheim that their opening number set the audience up for an evening about love being in the air instead of the broad farce that the show really was. The change was made, the show instantly began working like gangbusters, and it went on, of course, to become a hit on Broadway.

So no one could accuse us of not availing ourselves of one of the best musical theatre minds anywhere.

Robbins came to a Saturday matinee early in the run and afterwards huddled with Grover and Mike Frazier in the rear of the orchestra. Not wanting to overwhelm him, Cadiff and I stood unobtrusively nearby listening. And I'm glad we did because otherwise I wouldn't have believed what Robbins' advice was.

His big "fix" for us was to cut the female lead and make the show a story about a writer and his typewriter. Huh? A writer and his typewriter? I couldn't believe this was happening. He comes to Washington and inspires Sondheim to write "Comedy Tonight" and now he comes to Washington and tells us to cut the female lead in favor of an inanimate object? Where is the fairness in this world, I wondered, for one of many times on this production.

Thanks to Roger Stevens, though, there was one change in the offing that I had been unsuccessfully lobbying Jerry Colker to make since Pasadena. In a second act number, Alex's girlfriend, Dana, informs him in a letter/song that she's pregnant. I thought it was a contrived, soap-opera device that wasn't needed. Roger had agreed with me, but still it was there.

Roger had also been lobbying Frazier, Dietz, and me to force a cast change. He had seen understudy Michelle Pawk go on in the role of Alex's agent one night and wanted to fire Antonia Ellis and put Pawk in the role instead. The rest of us knew the chaos that would cause given that Ellis was Mrs. Jerry Colker, and we more or less politely ignored him. Plus, Ellis was indeed competent in the part.

Finally, one day Roger called for a summit in his office with the rest of us. He insisted on at least one of those two changes being made or he wasn't continuing with the show. We informed Cadiff of the ultimatum and left the choice to him and Colker, knowing, of course, what it would be. The next day, Dana was no longer pregnant.

Our meetings in Roger's Kennedy Center office often included him forgetting exactly how much financing he had committed to the show. Or was this just a business ploy to make us sweat? He was showing his age at almost 78, so we could never tell for sure whether it was senility or caginess. But, at this point, if he didn't deliver the full $1 million we were counting on, the other three of us would be in huge personal financial trouble, me more so than Frazier or Dietz. Fortunately, Deborah Dixon, who was still his assistant, would gently remind him of what the agreement was.

The work on the show that was done in D.C. focused on making specific moments better, not doing wholesale surgery, which wasn't possible either practically or creatively, and which none of us thought was necessary regardless. During performances, I'd walk around the Kennedy Center terrace overlooking the Potomac and wonder how I'd ever get out of debt. I was already writing off the show's chances, and I knew I could still pull out and cut my losses to some extent. Yet for some reason I couldn't bring myself to do that.

The mood around the theatre was hardly somber, however. It was a happy company that had, for the most part, been together for a long time. There, naturally, though, had been a few cast changes along the way. Actor B.D. Wong had left the show after Pasadena when he was offered the lead – and career-making role -- in David Henry Hwang's play, "M Butterfly," which ironically was playing a pre-Broadway engagement in Washington at the National Theatre at the same time we were at the Eisenhower. Wong was one of the nicest actors I've ever worked with and fully deserved the success that play brought him.

One fun episode during our time at the Kennedy Center occurred on a stage manager's birthday. The guys in the cast and crew decided to give this easily embarrassed young lady a surprise gift in the Eisenhower Theatre green room. They brought her in and had her sit directly beneath the stately portrait of Mamie Eisenhower. And then a male stripper breezed in and, well, strutted his stuff right in front of her while she cowered in a half-shocked, half-bemused state. The image of a male stripper gyrating within inches of an overwhelmed young damsel while dignified Mamie stared down on it all is an image I don't think anyone in the room will easily forget.

Meanwhile, as often happens with companies on the road, the rumor mill was churning and the backbiting had started by the second week, especially at the watering hole that became the regular late-night hangout for most of us. One of the fastest-spreading rumors was that the married Cadiff was having an affair with a member of the company.

Frazier, our wonderful general manager Frank Scardino, and I would have breakfast with Cadiff every Saturday morning to discuss the priorities for the coming week. The Saturday after the rumor broke, Frazier wanted to confront him about it. Having known both Andy and his wife, Kay Walbye, for several years at this point, I had every reason to believe they had a very solid marriage and I tended to discount the scuttlebutt as just that. But, in the unlikely event it *was* true, I hadn't seen it interfering with his work on "Mail" and, besides, there would be nothing we could do about it.

Frazier did confront him, though, and Cadiff firmly denied it, even correctly naming the cast member who had started the rumor and told us about it. After the meeting, Scardino observed to

Frazier and me, "The kid's either telling the truth or he's one hell of a liar."

As we left Washington, Cadiff's integrity was the only thing I did have confidence in, as I had very little about what fate had in store for us back in New York.

We played a little over two weeks of previews at the Music Box Theatre, and the generously papered houses were mostly responsive. During performances it didn't have the "feel" of a flop, but deep down I knew it would be. And the sense I got on the "street" confirmed to me that I wasn't wrong.

Opening night brought such cute opening night gifts as letter openers. But the vibe in the theatre as audience and critics waited for the show to start was not an encouraging one. Critics slumped in their seats, looking as if they'd rather be anywhere other than here. Then, as I watched from my perch at the back of the orchestra, I saw Joel Siegel, the ABC-TV critic, get up from his seat, walk up the aisle, and head to the men's room...*during the opening number.* Millions of dollars and artists' careers and livelihoods on the line, and he goes to take a piss (or whatever) just as the show is *starting*. This was beneath unprofessional behavior.

For whatever reason, the deck was clearly stacked against us. I may never have been the show's biggest fan, but I didn't understand the abject hostility I sensed coming from the critics and the New York theatre establishment.

That hostility permeated the reviews that started coming in a few hours later. Our opening night party took place in the spacious Franklin D. Roosevelt Post Office on Third Avenue in midtown. I hadn't previously known that federal facilities could be rented out after hours, but it was obviously an appropriate venue. Our press agent, Josh Ellis, took me into the men's room to show me Frank Rich's *Times* review; when the news is bad, some flacks try to keep it quiet so as not to put a damper on the party. Of course, within minutes it becomes common knowledge anyway.

"Mail" was a show that needed the critics to create a buzz. And, as became apparent at the ad agency meeting the next morning, they sure did. But the wrong type. The reviews were unanimously lethal. Not only bad, but gratuitously nasty. It was as if we had committed some heinous crime against the critics' families. Just as the Los Angeles critics' euphoria had made no sense to me, neither did the New York reviewers' venom.

Curiously, none of this was emotional for me, the way the (much more successful) "3 Guys" opening had been; my heart was able to remain detached.

I was sure we'd all be in favor of closing immediately, but since we didn't already have a closing notice posted for the end of the current performance week, the unions required us to run through the following week. So we did, and sales were dismal. We had to keep papering the house to give the actors some living bodies to play to at every performance.

When it came time to decide about posting a closing notice for the end of that following week, and doing so seemed inevitable, Colker's father approached Frazier and me and offered to put up $100,000 to keep the show running a little longer to see if it caught on. I knew it wouldn't, and I argued to Frazier and Dietz that our priority at this point, if we had the money, should be to make an original cast album. And if we *didn't* have the money, we should close ASAP. But my partners wanted to accept the elder Colker's money and keep the show running at a sizeable weekly loss in the hope it would catch on with audiences. The problem was that, with every performance being heavily papered, when a person who had gotten in free enjoyed the show, that person would indeed spread positive word of mouth...and also tell people how they too could get free tickets. It became a vicious cycle.

Roger Stevens by now had faded out of the picture and was in the process of turning over the chairmanship of Kennedy Center to retiring Time, Inc. chairman Ralph Davidson, whose brief and uneasy tenure in the position (a little over a year) would stand in stark contrast to Stevens' over-quarter-century as founding chairman appointed by JFK in 1961. Even though the Kennedy Center, as a 501(c)(3) not-for-profit corporation, was protected against loss beyond its sizeable original investment, I actually missed the seasoned perspective that Roger frequently brought when he was lucid. Davidson only attended one meeting (the day after the opening), and it was clear that he was out of his element.

So we ran another two weeks on the strength of Jack Colker's money, and business only kept getting worse. As we entered the last week in which it would cover most of the losses, I felt it was way past time for us to get out of Dodge. But the Tony Award nominations were being announced early the following week, and Frazier and Dietz wanted to hang around through that week to see what "Mail" might receive and whether that would spark business.

To my mind, this was beyond insane, and I finally found it within me to say "no." I distributed a signed letter withdrawing from the partnership, thus protecting myself from further loss. The box office grosses were going steadily down, and I knew any nominations we got wouldn't have an impact. With "Phantom of the Opera" and "Into the Woods" in position to walk away with the majority of nominations and awards, maybe we'd get two or three nominations in secondary categories, but we would clearly be an "also-ran."

Frazier went to the Tony nominations announcement ceremony the following Monday, and when I spoke to him from my self-exile when he returned, he was furious.

"Not a damn one," he angrily exclaimed. My first thought was that pulling out when I did had been the smartest move I had made since Pasadena. It ended up saving me tens of thousands of dollars, although I was still left with six figures of debt.

When I saw the full nominations list, I was incensed too, but not for quite the same reasons. So much of it defied any logic whatsoever. The musical "Chess" had also been one of that year's openings, and, though its production had been roundly criticized, it was trying to make a go of it next door to us at the Imperial. Abba's score for "Chess" might arguably have been the best score of the entire *decade*, with both a hit album and single. *And the Tony nominating committee totally overlooked it.* I mean, come on; no one's taking anything away from Sondheim or Lloyd-Webber, but how could an entire committee not recognize the brilliance of the score to "Chess" and give it one of the two remaining nomination slots for best score? Unlike us, it got a few best actor nominations, but its most outstanding asset was inexplicably ignored.

As for "Mail," the one nomination I felt was certain was Grover Dale's energetic, original, and sometimes even *funny* choreography. Nope. "Into the Woods," with very little choreography, got one instead. It was as if we didn't exist.

The truth is that Broadway didn't *need* us that season, and obviously didn't want us. Again, I had never been one of the show's true believers, but I also knew I had seen a lot of lesser shows be accorded more respect than we got. Had this been the type of paltry season Broadway was having in 1984-85, when "3 Guys" opened off-Broadway, it might have been a different story, but in this season, forget it.

Why then did we open when we did? The answer has to do with the realities of commercial theatre. Once we cranked up the machinery at the Kennedy Center, the "meter was running" and it would have been prohibitively expensive to shut everything down and wait for the following season. We had to either keep on going to the final destination or close for good. A lengthy hiatus would also have meant losing some cast members and having to rehearse the show all over again, an undesirable prospect creatively as well as financially.

"Mail" did finally close after the Tony snub. I felt nothing. And for some reason, the huge debt I had incurred due to a combination

215

of my morals and my desire for a Broadway opening didn't give me sleepless nights, even if I had no idea at the time that I would be able to pay it off easily within the next five years.

I knew that the economics of theatre had gotten too out of control for producers who weren't independently wealthy or had corporate affiliations and I accepted the reality that I couldn't afford to produce another show in New York theatre. So I moved to Los Angeles and was fortunate to be able to find a degree of success in television, having already started my transition into it a few years before. The principles of producing are the same as in theatre, the only difference being you get paid handsomely for doing it as opposed to having your financial life on the line with each new project. Still, theatre would always be my first love.

I wasn't the only "Mail" alumnus who re-located to Southern California. Cadiff and his soon-to-be second wife moved there as well. Yes, the rumors in Washington had been true. As we had become close friends over the previous five years, he apologized for having lied to me in D.C. He felt that had he confided in me, it would have put me in a horrible position as to whether I was obligated to tell my producing partners. I realized he was right; I was better off not knowing, and I forgave him.

Much as I had given Cadiff his breaks in New York theatre, Scott Bakula gave him his big break in television. The recognition – and living – that Cadiff couldn't find in theatre was quick to come in the L.A. tv world. In no time, he vaulted to A-list status among sitcom directors and never looked back, even as the quality of the shows he was working on began declining after a while. Sitcom directors are notoriously overpaid for the usually limited creative function they serve, subjugated as they are in that medium to producers and writers, and Andy wasn't the first to be seduced by the luxurious lifestyle Hollywood was bestowing upon him. Ironically, while I realized that trying to make a living in commercial musical theatre directing was no longer a viable alternative for him, I often felt as if I was observing the second act of "3 Guys Naked" in real life.

Cadiff drifted away from our friendship and I haven't heard from him in almost three decades. I hear he's now on his fourth wife and still toils in the sitcom world, although not at the high-quality level he once did. I won't pass judgment on his personal choices here, but I will say that musical theatre lost a director who I firmly believe would have made a mark as a major talent *had Broadway still been what it was* when we first became attracted to it in our teens. But this is what happens when an industry can't provide enough opportunities for its up-and-coming – and genuine – talents to stay financially afloat while pursuing their dreams.

I haven't returned to producing theatre, but I did come back to the east coast after nearly a decade in La La Land. I like to say that I moved out there to restore my bank account…and I moved back to restore my soul.

The Secret Service Plays Broadway

Throughout my years living in Los Angeles, I would fly back east for a week every May to see the slew of recently opened shows that had garnered Tony nominations so I could complete my awards ballot in good faith.

On these trips, I would always stay with Dennis Green and he'd accompany me to the shows. But the late afternoon I landed at Newark Airport in 1994, I didn't have time to stop at his apartment first and instead met him at the Palace Theatre where we were to see "Beauty and the Beast" that night. I had managed to pack economically for the trip, so it was easy enough to simply put my small suitcase under my seat at the theatre.

Tony voters are always given prime seats and ours were about six rows back in the center orchestra. As the house lights started to dim, Dennis and I heard a rumbling in the audience as four people hurriedly came down the aisle and took their seats in the row directly behind us,

We did double-takes when we realized who was sitting behind Dennis. It was former President George H.W. Bush. The woman he came with (not Barbara) was in the seat behind mine.

During the first act, I pretty much forgot they were there, except when the ex-president would comment to her on the show, which he did repeatedly and audibly.

"Amazing staging," he said at one point.

By then, I wanted to turn around and go "Ssssh!," but I thought better of it.

I was actually more bothered by the placement of the new songs that Tim Rice had written with Alan Menken. In some cases, they were both superfluous and damaging to the show's structure. And Howard Ashman would have hated them. Had he still been alive, I knew the stage musical would have retained and maybe built upon the animated film's integrity and not merely served to maximize marketing of the brand. True talents, as Julie Taymor showed four years later with her stage adaptation of "The Lion King," can do both in ways that are unique to the stage.

Regardless, they had a happy customer in Poppy Bush.

When intermission arrived, I stood up and started to make my usual trek to the lobby and men's room, as did Dennis. But suddenly the Secret Service was surrounding the area, one of them standing to my left and a few more in the center aisle where a steady stream of humanity was making its way toward the former president, hoping to get an autograph. We realized we weren't going anywhere right then.

After Bush had signed a dozen or so Playbills and with the line still endless, Dennis leaned over to him and jokingly said, "I bet whoever got you these seats is going to be fired first thing Monday morning!"

Not getting the humor of Dennis' remark, Bush replied pleasantly, "No, we really like these seats."

I accepted our fate that we were stuck right where we were for the rest of intermission, trapped in this vortex of humanity. So I struck up a conversation with the Secret Service agent who was standing within arm's length of me and looking bored. He was – big surprise – actually responsive, if somewhat guarded. But then I think I caught him off-guard.

"There's something I don't get," I said. "Here I am sitting only a few feet away from the guy you're protecting and I have a small suitcase under my seat that no one even looked twice at when I entered the theatre. I just walked right in with it."

He looked at me like the proverbial deer caught in the headlights as he thought of how to respond.

Finally, he shrugged and said something that caught *me* off-guard:

"Oh, well, he's not president any longer."

The League That Wouldn't Shoot Straight

It was Tony-voting season again and for the first time in a decade I was able to attend Broadway's eligible plays and musicals by driving in from New Jersey rather than flying in from Los Angeles. Throughout that spring of 1999 (the time of year when the vast majority of new shows invite Tony voters), the proximity of the street I loved was tempting me back, although where or how I'd fit in now was an unanswered question in my mind. Meeting up with old friends and colleagues might give me some ideas, though.

One evening, on the sidewalk outside the Brooks Atkinson Theatre (now the Lena Horne Theatre), where the Kevin Spacey revival of O'Neill's "The Iceman Cometh" was playing, I ran into Richard Frankel, whom I had known and always liked from his days as managing director of Circle Repertory Company. We arranged to have lunch one day soon.

I had always admired Richard and was pleased that he was becoming a force on Broadway. I was interested to find out how he, not being a wealthy person, had found a way of navigating his way through the economic straits that had become prohibitive for producers like me.

We met at his office where he showed me around. It was soon evident to me that the key to his survival was the general management side of his business, which was representing several clients (i.e., shows) at any given time. This provided him with a stable base, but I realized that it wasn't a path I could emulate given my decade-long absence and lack of interest in general management matters.

At his suggestion, for lunch we went to an upscale seafood restaurant looking down on Duffy Square. It was good catching up with him and reconnecting, even if the restaurant was grossly overpriced and he stuck me with the three-figure check without even suggesting we split it. When we left, we agreed to stay in touch, and he went off to an afternoon meeting, which I would later learn was a formal meeting of the 24-member board of governors of The League of American Theatres and Producers (which has since been renamed The Broadway League).

Little did I remotely imagine that he would be one of 23 votes at that meeting to strip over 100 producers of their long-standing privileges of membership. Including me.

But it wasn't long before I found out. The annual membership renewal letter from the League arrived in my mailbox soon thereafter. But it was longer than usual and buried in the middle of the five pages was the news that all members who had produced or managed a Broadway show within the past four years would be entitled to receive tickets to every eligible show and to vote on the Tony Awards.

Where did this arbitrary criteria come from? The rules had always been that once someone qualified for full membership, they were a full member for life as long as they paid the annual dues.

It was clearly a purge, but why was it happening?

I called Karen Vock, who was membership secretary at the League, and asked if I was reading this renewal letter correctly. She said I was and seemed very sympathetic to the feelings of those impacted. I asked if she could fax me a list of all the members whose rights were being taken away and she said she would.

The list came through and I read it over, astounded. Some of the names on it were Gail Berman Masters, who at the time was president of Fox Television Network; Doris Cole Abrahams, who had produced "Equus" and "Travesties"; David Brown, who had co-produced Broadway plays such as "A Few Good Men" and films such as "Jaws" and "The Sting"; Maurice and Lois Rosenfield, producers of musicals such as "Barnum" and the stage adaptation of "Singin' in the Rain"; and many others, along with a huge swath of less notable names.

Realizing that most people don't even bother to read what they think are boilerplate letters and simply pony up their dues, I put together my own letter advising others who had been sneakily disenfranchised of their fate and stating how wrong it was. The list that Vock had provided me included fax numbers for the members, so I sat at my fax machine one night drinking several vodka and tonics and faxing my letter to all 100-plus on the League's hit list.

I finally went to sleep just before the sun rose and, when I woke up, both my answering machine and my incoming fax tray were full. I had hit a nerve, and realizing that, without Tony-voting privileges, their League memberships offered them zero benefits, the disenfranchised members were in a fighting mood. I spent the day connecting with each of them. Within a week, we had an armada of over 60 targeted League members who were fuming and wanted to fight.

If you recall, I said there were 24 League governors and 23 votes to constructively terminate us. I learned that the one who voted against this move was my old friend Norman Rothstein. I called Norman and he filled me in on some of the details. Apparently, longtime producer and general manager Manny Azenberg was the one who had spearheaded this assault. Word had spread that he was angered over what had happened with that season's Tony Awards when his stunning production of "The Iceman Cometh" and its star, Kevin Spacey, had lost the Best Revival of a Play and Best Actor Tonys to the equally stunning production of "Death of a Salesman" and its star, Brian Dennehy.

This alone, however, wouldn't have explained it. Nothing is done in the League without the Shuberts' blessing and it was fairly obvious that Azenberg had Bernie Jacobs' and Gerry Schoenfeld's. Norman urged me to look at who had been admitted to the League in the last few years. More and more "road presenters" had been added to the membership roster and would continue to be. These are the people who operate and book theatres around the country, mostly with touring musicals. And the theory was that they would be inclined to vote to award Tonys to shows most likely to play in their theatres whereas the "deadwood old farts," as Azenberg was quoted as having called us, would be more inclined to vote our conscience. Understand, this is a rational theory of the motive, but there's no proof of it, and all that the governors needed to know when they voted was that Bernie and Gerry had approved if not initiated it.

Regardless of the politics, though, a situation was being created whereby (literally) the kid booking shows to play one night at Arizona State University would have a vote in the Tony Awards but the president of Fox Network would not.

Most sadly, Norman was dealing with a terminal cancer diagnosis at the time and, very understandably, didn't want his final days to be spent fighting the League. He died a few months later. It was a personal loss for me and a profound loss for the industry.

I knew that if we were going to fight our constructive termination, we'd need an attorney. Of course, we couldn't look to any of the established entertainment attorneys' firms to represent us against the League because none of them, with futures to protect, would want to be in an adversary position to the Shuberts. We finally landed a firm in northern New Jersey, and specifically a lawyer who was fascinated with the workings of the theatre industry. He was skeptical that we could prevail because the League is a private membership organization and was legally within its rights, but he was willing to try because he thought what they did was wrong.

My argument was that, while it might be a private membership organization, the attempt to manipulate the Tony Awards vote impacted the public interest, as most theatregoers make their buying decisions based on a show's stature and image, and winning Tonys enhances both.

Plus, the whole thing just didn't smell right. If they'd seek to taint the awards process, what else might they be doing? The very structure of the League is built on the faulty assumption that producers have the same interests as theatre owners. The bottom-line truth is that the former are in the entertainment business and, cosmetics aside, the latter are in real estate. In fact, each show has to negotiate its own deal with the theatre owner, and some of the terms can vary widely from deal to deal depending on which party has the greater leverage. But when the theatre owner is also one of the producers, as is common these days, the leverage can shift dramatically. Regardless, due to theatre owners being a source of investment for producers, no one has challenged, or is likely in the foreseeable future to challenge, the League structure.

I knew we were embarking on a David vs. Goliath battle, but I was encouraged by a note I received in the mail soon after word of our challenge spread. It was from an "A-list" power player on Broadway saying he was fully supportive of what we were doing. He had been unhappy with how the Tonys had been run in recent years and he saw our exile by the League as making it worse. He wanted to buttress our movement by working "behind the scenes," and, in order to do that, he asked that I keep his identity a secret. I referred to him as our "Deep Throat"...not original, but spot-on applicable.

Anyway, on behalf of our disenfranchised member group, I had two early meetings with Jed Bernstein, who was executive director of the League then, each time with fellow castrated League member Bob Blume, who was executive producer of the annual Drama Desk Awards. Bernstein was both cold and indifferent, stating that what was done was done. I maintained that if the League insisted on that as its policy going forward, then at least all current members should be grandfathered since they had joined with the understanding that they would have the full benefits of lifetime membership as long as they paid their annual dues. Or, at the very least, notice of a policy change should be given to existing members several years in advance of the implementation date, not furtively buried in the body of a membership renewal letter with the intent for it to go into effect immediately.

I pointed out to him that, as a member of the television academy as well, I could state that it didn't discriminate against *its* members in this way.

"Then why don't you just go back to television?" was Bernstein's arrogant reply.

(It should be noted that in the intervening quarter-century, the Academy of Television Arts & Sciences has changed some of its membership rules as well.)

Bob Blume and I brought Fred Zollo with us to our second meeting with Bernstein. Zollo was one of the new breed of producers who was more prolific than most, had a high profile within the League, and also believed that the organization had erred by purging members. We thought he might have greater influence than we did. He didn't. It was essentially a rerun of our first meeting.

While this was going on, our attorney had sent two letters to the League's attorneys (the Proskauer firm, as high-powered as they come) requesting documents. Chief among them was a list of eligible Tony voters from the past season. I had reason to believe that it would show the League to be in violation of its own bylaws that gave each theatre-owning entity (Shubert, Nederlander, Jujamcyn) a limit of four executives/employees it could designate as Tony voters. I strongly suspected that the Shuberts had more than that.

All of our attorneys' requests were denied.

That left us no choice but to take the League to court.

I strategized that it would be enough to fire a legal warning shot across their bow and file what's called an Article 78 proceeding. Essentially, for our purposes, this is a filing to a New York court by a member (or members) of an organization to get an order allowing for the examination of specified documents in the organization's files. At this point we were incurring fairly substantial legal fees, so I asked each member of our initiative to write a $500 check payable to our attorneys and mail it to me for transmittal. Within a week we had put together almost $20,000, and our attorneys were drafting our Article 78 action.

I received a call from Maurice Rosenfield, who was a wealthy Chicago civil rights attorney before he added Broadway producing to his caseload. He was happy to put in his share, but he strongly urged that we forget about taking a shot across the bow and proceed directly to a full-fledged lawsuit against the League. His argument was that we had momentum on our side now and that if too much time passed, the passion would fade.

After discussing it with our principal attorney and my attorney-wife (who had been wonderfully assisting *pro bono* throughout), as well as several of our activist group, it became clear that going the Article 78 route seemed the wiser, less expensive, and more practical choice at this juncture. We also felt it would strengthen our ultimate case if, with further exploration, we could uncover some truly damning evidence, which we thought we could.

We had become a nuisance to Bernstein and the League, but we sensed they didn't believe we'd litigate. They were wrong. After several months of back-and-forth, when it was clear that further discussions and document demands would yield nothing, we filed the Article 78 complaint in New York County Supreme Court. (In New York, rather oddly, Supreme Court is the trial court, not the highest appeals court.)

Three members of our group were named plaintiffs: Gail Berman, the aforementioned president of Fox Network; Seth Schapiro, the former Jujamcyn attorney; and me. One of us had to "sign off" on the complaint for it to be filed, and since I was geographically the closest to the attorneys' offices, it fell to me to do so. That meant the case would henceforth be formally known as *Wells v. League of American Theatres and Producers* even though I was not the sole plaintiff.

The thing about filing an action in court is that all else stops until a decision is rendered. It becomes a waiting game and you either focus on other things that matter in your life or you lose your mind.

December passed.

January passed.

As the proverb goes, the wheels of justice turn slowly. At least updates and encouragement from Deep Throat about what he called our "pincer movement" kept arriving regularly in my snail mail.

February passed.

Then on March 4th, 2000, the court's decision finally arrived. We had won on almost all points.

The most important document that the court ordered the League to turn over to us was indeed its full Tony voter list from the prior season. One would think it would be a document that the League would have in its computer files and be able to access quickly since the producer or general manager of every Tony-eligible production is sent a copy so they can invite Tony voters. But such was not the case. Days turned into a week and still nothing.

In what was obviously a slip, one of the Proskauer associates responded to our attorney's verbal query about its whereabouts by saying that the League was almost finished constructing it.

Huh? Did he have any idea he was giving credibility to our suspicions?

Finally, the League complied with the court order and sent us a list.

A general manager of Tony-eligible show from the prior season had already shared the list *he* received from the League at the time his show was inviting voters.

They didn't match. Names of some executives in the employ of theatre owners were missing from the League's list but were on the actual one from a year before.

We wanted to be doubly certain, though, so we got a list from the producer of a Tony-eligible production that had opened much later in the prior season than the one whose voter list we already had. I drove into the city and picked it up from his office.

Bingo. It was different than the other one we had, but only in that it reflected seemingly legitimate minor changes in membership. The names that represented violations of the League's own by-laws were still there.

I drove straight to our lawyers' offices, plopped the lists on our principal attorney's desk, and said, "Here's your smoking gun."

We now felt we had a solid basis to argue that the League had falsified a document that it had been forced to provide under court order. We also concluded that any cause of action we filed against the League needed to also name Bernstein himself as a defendant.

I strongly believed that this would be sufficient for a case filed by us to survive the standard and inevitable "motion to dismiss" that Proskauer would surely file in response. And if we did and were accordingly granted legal access in discovery to the League's records, I was confident that they'd approach us wanting to settle. My sense was that there'd be no way they'd want us digging through their records and learning all about what went on there.

Even though he had resigned from the League years before over other issues, Deep Throat agreed with this assessment and was, as ever, encouraging me to press forward.

By this point, taking note of our persistence and determination, the League had begun making moves of its own to counter us. Most significantly, its board of governors voted to amend the terms of the Tony-voting exclusion it had adopted the prior June. Its first move was to grandfather all of those affected who had been League members for 25 years or more. This gave full rights back to over a dozen of our group. Among them was Seth Schapiro, which meant they had knocked off one of our three named plaintiffs. Regardless, we viewed this as an initial victory, in that the League was responding to our pressure.

Sadly, though, there was a downside. Perhaps it's human nature, but, other than Seth, I never heard again from any of the others who had had their voting rights restored. So much for being in this together; they had gotten what they wanted for themselves, and the others who had helped them get it be damned.

In terms of the continuing legal maneuvering, it was time for a major summit with the League's attorneys and Bernstein to inform them of what we had and what steps we were prepared to take. For this meeting, I asked my old friend Ray Larsen to accompany our two lawyers (three if you include my wife) to the meeting. Ray was one of the people who had originally been on the list to have his voting rights rescinded, but he got a reprieve when he became a co-producer of the play "Copenhagen," which was coincidentally scheduled to open on Broadway that very night, April 11, 2000.

The League had two of its Proskauer attorneys, Jeff Horwitz and Mike Sword, present, as well as Bernstein, Karen Vock, and its then-President, Cy Feuer, a legendary producer (in partnership with Ernest Martin), most of whose Broadway work had been in the 1950s and 1960s (but who hadn't done a show since the late 1970s). Ironically, my mother-in-law had once been his theatrical attorney, but this was not the right occasion to bring that up.

We had sensed all along that Vock was sympathetic to our cause and that was confirmed by the look on her face when I referenced Ray as someone who would have lost his voting rights had he not liked "Copenhagen" and joined its producing team.

Both sides dug in and no progress was being made toward a resolution. Proskauer's Horwitz said he still didn't understand what the legal basis would be for a suit and our principal attorney, who I had come to realize was more of a schnauzer than a pit bull, left it to me to throw the grenade we had just been provided.

"We can now show that you were operating in violation of your own by-laws and that you had provided false documentation under court order."

The Proskauer attorneys and Bernstein erupted in a chorus of denials.

The meeting dissolved, with the League and its representatives furious at us for alleging that they had been anything less than candid and forthright.

Obviously at this point any more negotiating would be futile, so our choices were to file a full-blown lawsuit or do nothing.

The League had continued giving dispensations to certain long-term members who had not quite reached the magic 25-year mark. What this meant, combined with the earlier grandfathering, was that while we had won a partial victory, our troops were being significantly depleted. This meant that the amount needed to file a full-blown suit would be greater for each remaining plaintiff, both named ones and "et al."

The suit was almost completely drafted by this point, but we calculated that each remaining member of the plaintiff group would have to cough up an additional $2,000 or so to cover our legal fees to file and advance through the first phase of the litigation. Two grand was hardly a prohibitive amount, but an interesting and unexpected phenomenon had begun penetrating our ranks.

It was the middle of Tony-voting season again and many of those who had been purged discovered they didn't miss being part of it. And, truth be told, I didn't either. While having that status may seem glamorous from the outside, it often becomes an annual chore to those who have it. Tony voters who follow the stated rules (which isn't everybody) must have seen every nominee in a category before casting a vote in that category. This effectively means seeing almost *everything* that opens on Broadway and seeing most of it in a compressed period in the spring. The ugly truth is that the majority of those shows range from tolerable to painful. Sure, it's nice to have prime seats to the season's hit shows, but those comprise a very small percentage of the ones that open. And, as if to help this realization hit home, the 1999-2000 Broadway musical season was one of the weakest ever.

Our initial furor had been generated by the fact that something we were awarded upon joining the League, and which most of us had held for at least a decade, had been arbitrarily taken away from us. Ten months later, people had moved on with their lives and realized that they didn't really miss what had been taken from them.

Time had proven Maury Rosenfield correct. We shouldn't have wasted months on an Article 78 proceeding; we should have gone straight for the jugular when our passions were high. Legal machinery usually moves far too slowly to rectify injustices in a timely manner, and this is especially true in professional theatre.

We never did find out what the real motive for the League's once-in-a-century purge was, but if the rumor that it was an attempt to stack the Tony-voting to favor shows that would have the best touring prospects is true, it turned out not to be foolproof. Several times in the ensuing seasons, shows that have not been the most tour-friendly of the ones nominated have ended up receiving the best musical Tony, such as when "Avenue Q" upset "Wicked" four years later.

For me, this fight had always been primarily about principle, not tickets and voting rights. I wasn't bothered in the least by being perceived as the instigator of this challenge to the League and then its primary irritant.

One time, years before, I and several others had been bumped at the gate from an overbooked flight. When it was clear that no alternative flight was available that day, I started rallying everyone who had been bumped into a loud protest. A gate agent, realizing that I was creating a problem for her, approached me and whispered, "If we get you on the flight, will you go?" I nodded and followed her to the jetway, leaving my compatriots stranded.

I have felt guilty about that in the decades since and, in our fight with the League, I determined early on that if Bernstein or the League's governors tried that tactic with me, I'd refuse. They never did, but it helped me to better understand those who departed our ranks when they were offered the material benefit they sought.

This wasn't the way I had ever envisioned my association with Broadway theatre ending, but end it did following the 1999-2000 season, my last as a League member.

And, other than feeling a moral obligation to attend Deep Throat's (disappointing) musical retrospective of his career that the non-profit Manhattan Theatre Club presented in 2017, I have not set foot in a Broadway theatre since.

And One for Mahler

And One for Mahler

On the all-too-infrequent occasions when I share a meal with friend, drama critic, and walking theatre encyclopedia Peter Filichia, he more often than not reminds me of something I said to him back in 1975 as my first New York show was about to go into production.

I don't recall being so prescient, but apparently I said that this would undoubtedly be the only show I ever did on which I would be the sole producer above the title.

Whenever Peter reminds me of how true my prophecy was, we always segue into a discussion of how we both wish we had been born 20 years earlier. There was so much theatre we would have loved to have seen and experienced first-hand. Broadway and its denizens seemed to have so much character and verve. It was a world I wanted to be part of.

Somehow we were aware back then that we were coming in at the tail end of a golden era. What we didn't realize was just how radical the change would be in the coming years and decades.

Which leads me to acknowledge the sad truth that had the New York theatre world been then what it is now, I never would have wanted to be part of it.

Filichia and I may have agreed back in the '70s that the days of one producer or producing team above the title were numbered, but we never envisioned that half a century later there would ever be a musical with, by my count, 54 producers, as one Broadway show had recently. (Of course, they all aren't *really* producers; they're mostly investors, who used to be called "angels" and wouldn't receive billing.)

We surely couldn't have foreseen that the cost of producing a Broadway musical would be in the tens of millions of dollars. Or that it would cost hundreds of dollars for an orchestra seat to see a Broadway show.

Or, most crucially, that far too often the quality of the show you pay that much for is mediocre or worse.

Sure, there have always been Broadway shows that are painful to sit through, but it's one thing when you've spent $50 for a misfire of an evening and quite another when you've laid out $500.

Hal Prince foresaw the super-inflationary path that Broadway was on and in the mid-1970s began to move away from producing in order to concentrate on directing, and then completely abandoned his producer role in the mid-'80s. Even earlier, in a 1971 interview he granted me for my college newspaper, *The Cavalier Daily*, he prophesied the inevitability of Broadway one day being almost exclusively populated by non-profit theatre companies. We're not at that day yet by any stretch, but with three long-established 501(c)(3) companies – Manhattan Theatre Club, Roundabout, and Second Stage – now permanently occupying theatres on Broadway, I can't help but recall his words.

It also prompts me to think of the road I didn't take. When we opened the "new" WPA Theatre so successfully in the fall of 1977, I could have capitalized on it by hiring a personal PR agent to promote me as a significant new producing force in New York theatre at the tender age of 27. I could have committed myself to my Producing Director role, with fund-raising made easier by my higher industry profile, and simply put my personal frustrations aside for several years while I built on that profile. Sooner or later, I likely would have received an offer to head up a major non-profit, thus entering the arena from which top industry positions are filled.

There are several problems with that scenario, though. First, at the time, Broadway was the pinnacle and I wanted to be there ASAP. And second, I was neither given to self-promotion nor to thinking I had achieved anything so far worthy of undue recognition. Only in retrospect do I realize how extraordinary it was for someone in his twenties to do what I had done, most of all in establishing a much-lauded not-for-profit theatre company *in New York* that would have a lifespan of more than 25 years and that would launch many hit plays and successful careers. Not bad for five years out of college. But I didn't think that then.

Perhaps it was the lingering influence of my hateful stepmother, who always made me feel inferior, but at the time my self-appraisal was that I hadn't yet fulfilled my own expectations. I was still searching for contentment, both professionally and personally.

Another problem with the road I didn't take, of course, is that I wouldn't have had the experiences I *did have* that are meaningful to me and shaped my life today. Plus, I think, had I taken that road, I inevitably would have ended up being frustrated aesthetically. Which begs the larger question: Why are there no great dramatists today? The Millers and Inges, the Kauffman & Harts and Simons have left no successors.

What has evolved is a theatre whose writers tend to be preoccupied with The Human Condition, The Black Experience, The Social Guilt of the Day, and other such lofty concerns. All of which is fine, if they also adhered to the established precepts of American drama: compelling characters interacting and confronting a conflict *in an entertainingly dramatic or comedic way.* But instead, we have "slice of reality" plays.

I recall sitting in the old Morosco Theatre when I had just turned 18 and being spellbound and emotionally invested as the original production of Arthur Miller's play "The Price" unfolded onstage. I likewise remember seeing all of Neil Simon's early comedies in the '60s and each time leaving the theatre having had a totally fulfilling and fun experience that I couldn't have had elsewhere.

It seems the very notion of a Broadway play being, above all, an entertainment, whether it have a larger social purpose or not, is a distant memory. And fun? Forget it. When was the last time, say, a new comedy-thriller in the vein of "Sleuth" or "Deathtrap" was presented on Broadway? Apparently, no one is writing them any longer.

But then, maybe worthy successors to the gifted writers of Broadway past *do* exist; they just haven't been drawn to theatre. Not only haven't there been enough exciting new plays to provide them with the inspiration to desire a career in theatre since the old Broadway faded away, but given the renaissance of television in the age of cable programming and streaming services, the upper tier of today's writers can find creative and financial fulfillment much more reliably there.

Which would you rather strive for, being a senior writer on an acclaimed series such as "Succession" and earning a few hundred thou a year, or writing a play basically "on spec" and, if it garners interest, then shepherding it through development and maybe regional productions for minimal royalties, with no assurance of making money even if does get produced commercially?

In the era of the great American playwrights, a play could fail and a gifted writer could have another one produced within the following year or two. Today, the costs and stakes on Broadway are so high that it's hard to overcome a failure. So many business and financial people in the industry want a star, a hot writer, a London hit, something that "guarantees" them success, same as Dick Wolff did back in my Jujamcyn days. What they don't realize is that there *are* no guarantees in theatre.

And the same way writers have moved away from theatre, so too have independent "creative" producers. After "Mail," I found my-self $150,000 in debt while making only $75,000 a year at King Features (The Hearst Corporation is notoriously cheap). I moved to Los Angeles the following year, and through a development deal in partnership with Doug Wyman at Castle Rock Entertainment and my senior producing position on a Family Channel series that had a four-year run, I was not only able to pay off my debt within three years, but also buy a large home in a beach community with a panoramic view of the Pacific within five years. Most importantly to me, by working with people who had a similar aesthetic, I was able to do so without sensing I had in any way compromised myself, a feat that's even easier to achieve today, some 30 years later, given the plethora of high-quality programming that narrowcasting brought with it.

My first passion was, and always will be, Broadway, or rather the Broadway that *was*. But even with my renewed solvency in the early '90s and the stock market boom of the mid-90s that I was fortunate to be able to benefit from, I knew Broadway producing had become such a high-stakes game that it was out of my league.

It was now becoming a game for wealthy entrepreneurs and corporations, the most conspicuous of the latter being Disney. And with the exception of Julie Taymor's exquisitely conceived adaptation of "The Lion King," the impetus for Disney's Broadway musicals has been about milking the popularity of its successful animated films, not about creating vibrant theatre. Howard Ashman himself would have told you to save your money, skip the clumsily adapted "Beauty and the Beast" on Broadway, and treat yourself to a repeat viewing of the brilliant animated film whose success it trades on. Disney's motive behind the Broadway "Beauty and the Beast" and most of its derivative musicals that followed was money, not creative inspiration.

This, of course, is fine with Broadway's biggest power players, the theatre owners. The Shuberts, Nederlanders, and Jujamcyns are, when it comes down to it, in the real estate business, not theatre. Like any landlord, they want and need a high occupancy rate, regardless (except in rare cases) of who it is. And, as I mentioned earlier in discussing the League, their priorities are not the same as those of producers. (But guess who dominates.)

For both, however, the sophisticated marketing techniques that have evolved over the last half century are something to celebrate. Indeed, marketing is the primary reason that some hit musicals now have runs of over 20 years when, historically, the longest running shows lasted maybe seven years or so. And it certainly isn't because shows like "Cats" and "Phantom of the Opera" are better than shows like "My Fair Lady" and "Fiddler on the Roof."

What's lost in all this, though, is the development of new musical theatre talent. There hasn't been a great songwriting team on Broadway since Kander and Ebb, or composer/lyricist since (arguably) Maury Yeston. I go back to the sight of Peter Larson in tears on the opening night of "Brownstone" in 1986; this is a guy who showed the potential to develop into a great composer, but whose dream died for reasons of survival and family responsibility when Frank Rich called his score "impersonally professional and forgettable."

Do I fault Rich? No, it's one man's opinion. I fault an industry that doesn't prepare for its own future. Neither Rich nor any *Times* theatre critic reviewing New York commercial theatre *asks* for the disproportionate negative power he or she has. But, once again, ask yourself: What other industry allows one person's opinion to so often be the determining factor in the fate of a new product?

While the power of the *Times* has always been a subject for Broadway folks to gripe about, like so much else in the industry nothing ever gets done about it. No, the answer is not for its critics to become more lenient in reviewing shows; if every review spins positive, then the reviews cease to have any meaning.

But neither the *Times* nor critics in general are responsible for the dramatic change in Broadway culture over my adult lifetime. Actually, nothing has truly changed when it comes to critics since the 1960s when New York daily newspapers began folding, leaving only three by the mid-'70s. What *have* changed, as I've discussed, are the economy and the media landscape.

Still, Broadway, which for generation after generation had been dubbed "the fabulous invalid," is, on the surface, perhaps healthier than ever. But with what quality of product and at what cost, I have to ask? And a fair answer might be that I haven't advanced with the times and that it's nothing new for people in their seniority to claim "things were better in the old days."

Maybe so, and if 50 or so "producers" find satisfaction in simply getting their names above the title on one show so most of them can tell their friends they produced it when they didn't, and if audiences really feel they're getting their (insane amount of) money's worth for what's being presented, then I'm happy for them. (This has always been a credo of Filichia's; if someone says they liked a show that he didn't, he sincerely tells them he's glad they did.)

But there's one element that, for the most part, has definitely been lost over the decades and it's *craft*, particularly where musicals are concerned. How many writers today would fully understand why "Part of Your World" couldn't be cut from "The Little Mermaid" film (which was structured as a stage musical would be, even if it was for animation) and have the confidence of his convictions to stand up to an industry power-player like Jeff Katzenberg, as Ashman did?

I remember how I began to learn, back when I was a teenager going to Broadway shows every weekend, usually with my mother. I'd see every musical on Broadway, and I'd actually learn more from the ones that didn't work than those that did. But how could most parents afford to indulge a kid's passion like that today? Since the price of Broadway tickets has skyrocketed at a much higher rate than that of inflation in general, it would certainly have been out of reach for my mother and most other parents as well. Hell, even now as a relatively affluent adult, if I had a desire to attend a Broadway show once or twice a week, it'd be pretty much out of my reach.

None of this means I don't still go to theatre. I just don't go to Broadway, or to any theatre that pays a stipend or percentage to The

Broadway League. It's a principled stand based on the 1999 purge. But my boycott doesn't extend to regional theatres, which I frequent when something appeals, nor to London's West End, which is the closest thing I know to what Broadway used to be.

Nothing in my life has replaced the Broadway I loved, but, curiously, I don't miss it very much. Or maybe it isn't so curious. It's hard to actively miss something that's no longer there as you knew it. Wistful, yes. But, more than anything, I'm sad, not for myself but for all the people who don't – and can't afford to – generically say "let's go to the theatre tonight" and *then* decide what to see, as true theatregoers used to. Now it's an "event" business.

Sure, I wish it hadn't changed, the same way I wish the television industry in the '80s and '90s had offered the multitudinous opportunities to do quality work that it does today. But, overall, I'm grateful to have been able to travel the road I did, without having to make any major compromise to my values. As a kid in college, I envisioned a future in which I would be heralded for the impact I'd be making in New York theatre. I can't say that ever happened, nor that it should have, but, looking back, I realize that I had the privilege of being accepted as the most important thing of all in the industry of my dreams.

A player.

Acknowledgments

Dennis Green used to joke that if he ever won an award, he already had his acceptance speech set to go.

"There are numerous people I would like to thank for helping me get this far in my career," he would say, with a piece of paper in his hand. "But then you know who you are. There are many more of you, though, who I would like NOT to thank and they are…"

With which he would let the paper he was holding unfold and reach all the way to the ground.

There's a lot of truth behind the humor he invoked to make his point. There are usually more people you encounter who don't believe in you than who do, more who throw obstacles in your way than who open doors or offer encouragement. Or, most painfully, once you're established, those *you* go out of your way to help but who, once *they're* established, arrogantly brush you off if you ask *them* for something.

However, there are always a handful of special people without whom your journey wouldn't have been possible and whose belief in you affirms your belief in yourself.

In my case, Howard Rogut was always there for me, both as my associate on "The Confirmation" and at Jujamcyn. (He might never speak to me again if, at this point, I don't share with you that to this day he remains Mary Martin's most ardent fan, a fact that anyone who meets him usually becomes aware of within the first five minutes.)

Without Howard's support from the inside, I doubt I would ever have landed at Jujamcyn, which re-ignited my career after the post-WPA lull. And it was always a joy to work with him and to know he'd be standing beside me even in the darkest moments.

Bernie Rosenberg only got one mention in the text of this book, but he was an extraordinary gentleman, the dean of Broadway accountants, and my guiding light in the business. I got to know Bernie after my first show had closed when he and I had to clean up a bureaucratic mess that the show's attorney had made with the New York State Attorney General's office. We instantly bonded and he soon became my personal accountant (as well as preferred show accountant) and, more importantly, friend. With his silver hair and broad frame, he was as gentle a man as I have ever met, as well one of impeccable integrity. I was honored that he thought I was worth his time, given the established heavyweight clients he had.

Bernie and I would meet for lunch once every month or two and exchange thoughts about developments within the industry. After "Mail" left me with sizeable debts to pay off, I didn't receive an invoice from him for preparing my personal taxes for the next four years. Every time I asked him for it, he'd tell me it's in the mail and then change the subject. When he knew I had paid off the debt and was back on my financial feet in a fairly substantial way, he sent me a bill for $10,000 for all those years, which I quickly and happily paid, along with a warm note acknowledging his act of kindness. Bernie retired in 2002 after more than 50 years in the industry. I was profoundly saddened when I learned of his passing in 2009 from Alzheimer's.

My first advertising rep, Mike DeLuise, became another good friend who was there for me at many turns during my time in New York theatre. One of the regrets I had about not being the sole producer on a show was having to share the selection of the support staff with my partners, which led to my working with several different general managers, press agents, attorneys, and ad reps. As it turned out, I didn't have as much opportunity to retain Mike's marketing services as I would have liked, but we remained close colleagues. He even introduced me to an investor he knew who put up the final portion of what "3 Guys" needed in order to finance its tryout in Chapel Hill, for which I will be forever grateful, especially considering he wasn't the ad rep on the show. I have re-connected with Mike in recent years and my life is richer for it.

Then, of course, there's Dennis himself, a recurring figure in this memoir, who I dragged into more ventures than I can count and who endured the eccentricities of many companies and producing partners I was involved with and did so with indefatigable good humor combined with a healthy dose of sarcasm. Not only is he a brilliant lyricist, but he's also been the best godfather to my two sons that any kid or parent could hope for. My wife, sons, and I all consider him a member of our family, and more one cannot ask for in what started over half a century ago as a professional relationship.

Much gratitude to Doug Wyman and Chris Auer, individually my former partners in television, for their substantive belief in me. Chris, being the biggest straight "show queen" I've ever known, was this memoir's biggest fan during its writing, and Doug, in his detailed editing suggestions, showed yet again why his mind is among the sharpest I've ever encountered. And to Jim Reagen, who graciously and tirelessly shepherded me through all aspects of the publishing process, which I chose to pursue to make sure the final product was exactly as I wanted it to be.

Lastly, to my wife of 33 years, Tracy, for keeping me on track every step of the way and for fulfilling the far larger dreams of my youth.